ENGLISH STAGE COMEDY

ENGLISH STAGE COMEDY

Edited with an Introduction by W. K. WIMSATT, Jr.

ENGLISH INSTITUTE ESSAYS · 1954

COLUMBIA UNIVERSITY PRESS

New York · 1955

124295

PE
1010
E5
1954

PUBLISHED IN GREAT BRITAIN, CANADA, INDIA, AND PAKISTAN

BY GEOFFREY CUMBERLEGE, OXFORD UNIVERSITY PRESS

LONDON, TORONTO, BOMBAY, AND KARACHI

MANUFACTURED IN THE UNITED STATES OF AMERICA

Library of Congress Catalog Card Number: 55-9066

EDITOR'S NOTE

The essays which make this volume are drawn from two series of conferences at the English Institute, that of 1953 on "Comedy as a Literary Form," directed by Professor Charles J. Hill of Smith College, and that of 1954 on "English Stage Comedy," directed by myself. The present volume thus illustrates for the first time the Institute's new plan of accumulating essays from one year to another to produce thematically unified volumes under special titles.

It is a pleasure to acknowledge the debt of the Institute not only to the six authors whose essays on stage comedy are here presented and to Professor Hill, but also to Professor James A. Work of Indiana University, and to Professor Edgar Johnson of The City College of New York, whose essays on "The Comic Vision of Laurence Sterne" and on "Dickensian Comedy" were part of the 1953 series. Not the least of the problems which the Institute's Supervising Committee encounters, as it seeks to work its way toward a program of more nearly self-sustaining publication, is the embarrassment of literary riches.

W. K. W., JR.

Silliman College, Yale University
January 10, 1955

✑ TEXTS AND ACKNOWLEDGMENTS

C. L. Barber in his essay on Shakespeare's *Henry IV* quotes from the Oxford text of W. J. Craig. Bernard Knox in his essay on *The Tempest* quotes from the *Variorum* edition of H. H. Furness (1892), with the exception that he adjusts *u* and *v, i* and *j* to conform to modern usage. With the same exception, Ray L. Heffner, Jr. in his essay on Ben Jonson quotes from the edition of Jonson's works by C. H. Herford and Others (Oxford, 1925–52).

The passages from T. S. Eliot in W. K. Wimsatt's introductory essay on "The Criticism of Comedy" and in William Arrowsmith's essay on "The Comedy of T. S. Eliot" are quoted by permission of Harcourt, Brace and Company, Inc., from *Four Quartets,* copyright 1943 by T. S. Eliot, *The Cocktail Party,* copyright 1950 by T. S. Eliot, and *The Confidential Clerk,* copyright 1954 by T. S. Eliot. Additional passages in Mr. Arrowsmith's essay are quoted from the second edition of *Selected Essays,* copyright 1934 by T. S. Eliot, by permission of Faber and Faber Limited. The passage from Mr. Eliot's *Poetry and Drama* (copyright 1951) is quoted with the permission of Harvard University Press, and the passage from Mr. Eliot's essay on "The Aims of

Poetic Drama" is quoted with the kind permission of the publishers of *Adam International Review*.

The passages from Bernard Shaw in Katherine Gatch's essay on "The Last Plays of Bernard Shaw" are quoted with the permission of the Society of Authors.

⤳ CONTENTS

ENGLISH STAGE COMEDY

W. K. Wimsatt, Jr.

ঙ INTRODUCTION: THE CRITICISM
OF COMEDY

Despite a classical tradition concerning miscarriage at the sight
of Aeschylean furies, or bad conscience laid open, and despite a
tearful indulgence that seems to have been fairly frequent with
audiences in the eighteenth century, tragedy is nowadays hardly
expected to produce even the commotion of tears. On the other
hand, one of the most patent facts about comedy is that even
the modern audience does laugh, and is apparently expected to.
One recent writer on the subject has indeed considered it "very
doubtful whether the end of comedy is to produce laughter." He
observes that "many of the greatest comedies have a rather sober-
ing effect." His argument may work especially well for the comic
novel or the "comic" essay. Mr. Potts may be able to read *Emma*
to himself without laughing.[1] But a comic play at which people
do not laugh sounds like an odd success, and this no doubt helps
to explain both why the literary comic tradition centers on the
stage, and why comic theory has almost always been implicated
in theory of laughter. The phenomenon of laughter does offer
an easily locatable, if perhaps only superficial, point of reference for talking about a literary species.

[1] L. J. Potts, *Comedy* (London, 1949), pp. 10, 19–20.

At the same time, laughter has always been one of the chief embarrassments of the comic theorist. Theories of laughter, by definition, or by initial assumption and focus, are of course just that—theories of the laughing person and his pleasure. It is possible to reduce the subjectivity of the theory even to a simple tautology, saying: To laugh at something is just to throw your laughter at it, thereby *making* it laughable. The laughable is just what you laugh at. And so have said such disparate figures as Samuel Johnson (in his *Rambler* 125) and Max Eastman (in his guidebook *Laughter*), the latter appealing to the psychology of MacDougall for the concept of an innate laughing impulse, a primary humorous instinct.

Even laughter theories of a more special content are not so various as might be feared. They are all subject-centered in a double sense, in that they all stress not only a subjective feeling but the aspect of an egoistic gratification. The essential is always some form of either "triumph" or "liberty." Thus Plato said in the *Philebu*s that stage comedies give us a malicious feeling of gratification at seeing bullies and braggarts revealed as harmless pretenders. And Hobbes conferred upon the early modern version of this theory the confident, bouncing name of "Sudden Glory." His formulation is always worth quoting:

> *Sudden Glory,* is the passion which maketh those *Grimaces* called LAUGHTER; and is caused either by some sudden act of their own, that pleaseth them; or by the apprehension of some deformed thing in another, in comparison whereof they suddenly applaud themselves. (*Leviathan,* i, vi.)

During the later nineteenth century the theory of triumph receives its crudification through various physiological, psychological, and primitivistic analogies: the expression of the suckling infant, the laughter of children in barbarous games, the roar of the savage in victory, the smile on the face of tiger or Cheshire cat.[2] A more complex modern version appears in the group of "oscillation" theories, which, beginning with the grossness of tickle, move toward the refinements of alternating emotions, attitude mixing, or mental hopping, and of correspondingly ambivalent objects—for example, the woman, towards whom we entertain dominant feelings of affection often interrupted by feelings of hostility.[3] Hence an experience of mental tickling and laughter, and hence all those jokes about women which the theorist, who is usually a man, remembers so vividly.[4]

Again, Plato in his *Republic* and *Laws* warns us that laughter is a dangerous kind of escape. And Shaftesbury, giving us a revaluation of the old idea, says laughter is a liberating force in political and religious debate and a kind of aid to finding the truth.[5]

> The natural free spirits of ingenious man, if imprisoned
> or controlled, will find out other ways of motion to relieve

[2] Cf. Jim Corbett, *Man-Eaters of Kumaon* (Oxford, 1946), pp. 97–98.

[3] See D. H. Monro, *Argument of Laughter* (Melbourne, 1951), especially pp. 214–19, 222–25, outlining the theories of Greig and Menon.

[4] If the notion of tickle is pursued in the direction of the physical stimulus, we can arrive at laughter as the subject of experiments with electric shocks to the muscles of the face. (One side smiles, the other does not, in a picture the caption of which should surely be "Funny as a Crutch.")

[5] Cf. A. O. Aldridge, "Shaftesbury and the Test of Truth," *PMLA*, LX (1945), 129–56.

themselves in their constraint; and whether it be in burlesque, mimicry or buffoonery, they will be glad at any rate
to vent themselves, and be revenged on their constrainers. . . .
'Tis the persecuting spirit has raised the bantering one.
(*On the Freedom of Wit and Humour,* i, iv.)

True, laughter as freedom or frivolity in politics is today only an
occasional subject of concern.[6] But laughter as personal liberty
has been much treated by psychological theorists. Certain very
generalized and softened speculations are urged, for instance,
by Auguste Penjon in the *Révue Philosophique* for 1893 and by
his follower L. W. Kline in the *American Journal of Psychology*
for 1907. A bit of bark in a fireplace blazes up, and persons seated
dreamily about the embers smile. A big drop of rain falls into
a pond, and boys sitting about gazing at the surface smile. Children snicker at nothing in the restraint of a school room. Spectators laugh at almost nothing in a court room. "The function
of the humorous stimulus consists in cutting the surface tension,
in taking the hide off consciousness." [7]

Can the triumph of laughter be distinguished from the liberty?
Everybody will think of Freud's *Wit and Its Relation to the*

---

[6] Consult, for instance, H. M. Kallen, "The Arts and Thomas Jefferson," *Ethics,*
LIII (July, 1943), 282; and T. V. Smith, "The Serious Problem of Campaign
Humor," *New York Times Sunday Magazine,* Sept. 28, 1952, p. 11. Jefferson
deplored the levity of the French and in 1789 worried about their capacity for a
serious revolution. The most insidious modern attempts with laughter are perhaps being made in the comic strips. "Beneath the high notes of patriotism, we
want to hear the low notes of laughter, always off-key, always true. Jagged, im-
perfect and lovely, the goal lies here. This is the estate of our independence"
(Walt Kelly, *The Incompleat Pogo* [New York, 1953], p. 191).

[7] "The Psychology of Humor," *American Journal of Psychology,* XVIII (1907),
433–36.

Unconscious—the polite aggression, often sexual, of the tendentious joke, the psychic economy or easy irrational leaps of idea which explain the pleasure of even the harmless joke, the dreamy art form of comedy where grownup people enjoy a regression to an infantile, arcadian *id* realm.

> The euphoria which we are thus striving to obtain is nothing but the state of a bygone time, in which we were wont to defray our psychic work with slight expenditure. It is the state of our childhood in which we did not know the comic, were incapable of wit and did not need humor to make us happy.[8]

In a book called *The Origins of Wit and Humour,* published as recently as 1952, Albert Rapp argues that laughter is a demobilization, a *relief* from tension, upon sudden *triumph,* and his archetype is the supposed mirthful guffaw of very early savage man enjoying a victory in hand-to-hand conflict. Hence the laughter of ridicule, whether spontaneous or incited by words, and hence too the laughter of wit, which has an intermediate ancestry in such mental tussles or riddlings as may at one time have taken the place of more savage physical strife. Seeing the point of a joke is enjoying a sudden mental triumph. Jokes about sex or about Prohibition in America thirty years ago are easily enough explained as triumphs over suppression. Perhaps Mr. Rapp has more trouble when he tries to incorporate into his system the very common form of laughter which he calls "loving ridicule," or humor. The laughter itself remains just as aggres-

[8] *The Basic Writings of Sigmund Freud,* trans. A. A. Brill (New York, 1938), p. 803.

sive as ever (the archetypal laughter of the mother at the child who toddles and falls, the laughter of the English audience at Falstaff), but in a happy transformation the selfish principle is fused, mixed, or merged with love. Thus a victory is gained by annexation or *Anschluss* with the opposing principle. The theorist has his own way by reasserting a definition. Laughter is just per se aggressive, no matter what you join with it, or in what nonaggressive forms it appears.

Why do I laugh when my opponent trumps his partner's ace? when the wind blows off the parson's hat? when an old blind peddler stumbles and spills his pencils all over the street? I don't know. Maybe I don't laugh. But a Fiji Islander would! He will laugh when a prisoner is being roasted alive in an oven! Confident proclamations about the nature of anthropoid laughter are invested with importance by equally confident assumptions that reduction to the lowest common factor is the right way of proceeding. Civilized society discourages cruel jokes and brutal laughter, but what primitive society does is more important. Not what I laugh at but what I don't laugh at is the critical clue to my laughter. Are such theories of hidden elements and forgotten origins supposed to increase my appreciation of jokes or comic situations? It would appear not. If I dwell on the explanations long enough, or let myelf pretend to believe in them, I begin to be conscious of a distinct aversion to laughter.

Here, at this terminus of sheerly affective theory about laughter, we are a long way from being able to frame any critical discourse about works of comic literary art. Happily, we may turn —or at least we may, with some effort, work our way—to another tradition.

The more austere theories which have looked away from the laugher himself, or out from his consciousness or unconsciousness as a laugher, toward the things he may be supposed to laugh at, have always laid stress upon some kind of contrast. The Kantian incongruity between idea entertained and sensuously discovered object and the similar formula of Schopenhauer are among the most purified versions.[9] Obviously the basic notion calls for some kind of subtilizing. Yet attempts to subtilize it have often enlisted the aid of some markedly affective clause, as in the "tickle" and "oscillation" theories, where we have noted already that some ambivalent figure like the woman is the cognitive counterpart of a certain supposedly rapid alternation of feelings.

Arthur Koestler's *Insight and Outlook* (1949), draws a "Geometry" of wit somewhat as follows: Imagine that there are "Operative Fields" of ideas (groups or systems of ideas that go together), and imagine two of these fields adjacent to each other, and a train of thought traveling through one of them. The thought comes to the border and happens to encounter there one of those double-faced symbols or ambiguities so prominent in wit-work of all kinds—a "bisociated" link between the fields. Quick as a flash the thought jumps from one field to the other. But a load of emotion which was being carried along—more physical, lumpish, inert—is jolted off and left behind or shot to one side, discharged (re-cathected, as Freud would say), sluiced off in laughter. And it is precisely the kind of emotion, the painful feeling of antagonism, which, being sidetracked by the witty

---

[9] *Critique of Judgment,* Book II, par. 54; *The World as Will and Idea,* Book I, chap. xiii.

jolt, determines the comic pleasure. If the emotion is of another sort, then the geometry of wit may just as well fit the case of "serious" poetry, or, for that matter, of scientific discovery. The thought structure is always the same. The emotions differ and determine comedy, tragedy, or science. Thus a resolute show of joining thought and emotion in the same diagram turns out to be a device of thoroughly affective implication.

More successful attempts to complicate a theory of ludicrous contrast have moved in the social and moral direction. The tradition begins when Aristotle observes that comedy deals with characters inferior to those in real life, but that the comic defect (*hamartēma*) is, unlike the tragic, not painful or destructive (*anōdunon kai ou phthartikon*), and perhaps there ought to be a happy ending. The latter clauses are the cognitive counterparts to a notion of laughter as a somewhat kindly movement. (On these clauses, in the long run, may well depend the most reliable kind of distinctions between the tragic and the comic.) Molière, Pope, Swift, and Fielding spoke much, in harsh and punishing tones, about certain vices, follies, affectations, and hypocrisies. But softer modern illuminations have occurred, as in German romantic criticism, or in Meredith's lecture (partly inspired by Jean Paul) celebrating the "thoughtful laughter" excited in a competent observer by the combat between the sexes in the high society game, or again in Bergson's view of the laughable as failure of the *élan vital,* the suspension of vitality in any form of mechanism or stereotype—the physical automatism of stumbling, for instance, or the mental rigidity of absent-mindedness or bad habits. (The comic character comes to

be seen as incapable of moving toward discovery of himself—
fixed in mere postures of self-exposure.[10]) Most recently appear
the refinements of Mr. Potts, though he does not believe in the
happy ending—nor in laughter, as we have seen. Aristotle said
that in tragedy the fable is the first principle; the characters
come in for the sake of the fable. He did not say the opposite
for comedy. But Mr. Potts is able to make it look as if indeed
he might have, as if a more or less necessary chain of temporal
events following on some blunder may be essential to tragedy,
while a "spatial" pattern of characters significantly opposed and
acting to reveal one another may be equally essential to comedy.
The action follows the free whim of the characters. The tragic
character is unusual but normal, whereas the comic character
is just the opposite, abnormal or eccentric, but all too usual
(as the psychologist tells us today that most persons are neu-
rotic). Comedy is the spirit of humility and of measurement by
the norm. Thus far Mr. Potts.

In the *Poetics* of Aristotle, comedy does not enjoy a mythic
status, for comedy is to deal not with heroes of myth but with low
characters. It seems certain enough that any further Aristotelian
remarks on comedy which may be lost did not argue a very
cogent relation between comedy and symbol. Metaphor was
for Aristotle a way of heightening poetic style—or it could be
a joke, if deliberately misused. But these facts in the history
of literary theory do not make it impossible that ancient comedy
should be found actually symbolic in structure, or even mythic,

[10] Cf. Maynard Mack, Introduction to Fielding, *Joseph Andrews* (Rinehart
Editions, 1948), p. xiv.

with "comic Oedipus patterns" and the like. At any rate, modern critics of myth and symbol (among whom Northrop Frye [11] enjoys an extremely advanced position) practice a hugely expanded analogical mode which embraces with equal confidence both tragic and comic and their origins in ritual death or ritual resurrection, heroic quest and divine sacrifice, or carnival misrule and the "green world" of Robin Hood. Albert Cook's *The Dark Voyage and the Golden Mean* (1949), dichotomizes all human experience into mutually dependent "antinomic symbols," the wonderful—instanced in the tragic quest—and the probable —instanced in the social norm from which the comic deviates into existence. Comedy and tragedy are part of an almost transcendental opposition which includes, at different levels, such various pairs as concept and symbol, sex and death, the beautiful and the sublime, success and failure, bourgeois and aristocrat. This kind of criticism seems as vastly removed as it is possible to be from all that concern with the convulsions of laughter and its stimuli which we encounter in Mr. Rapp and the other psychological writers. The structures of significance indeed are so manifold and so extensive that even a small incautious laugh here might set off thunderous and toppling reverberations.

We have been speaking about theories of laughter itself and then about theories of what is laughed at so far as these two may be separately discernible. It must be admitted, however, that laughter and the laughable are not often discussed separately for very long. (And here the critic's task is going to be greatly complicated—though at the same time his opportunities may be

[11] See *English Institute Essays, 1948,* ed. by D. A. Robertson, Jr. (New York, 1949).

marvelously enriched.) The two kinds of theory tend to come together—the automatized object of laughter in Bergson's theory, for instance, looking a great deal like the comatose or mechanized subject just before he is awakened by laughter in the theory of Penjon—the Platonic stage bully being, one fears, not so much unlike the ego of the audience which rises in the appropriate laughter of malice and triumph. There is much room in the laughing situation, much need, for "empathy." And this is especially true of the situation in comic art, for art is a reflexive work, a thing contrived of the human object only as this is caught in the light of responses thrown upon it. Comedy (to compress into one sentence a great deal that is important but in the climate of recent critical theory almost a truism) combines the accent of laughter and the accent of sympathy in a union of the laugher and his audience with the targets of laughter. Molière in his *Critique de l'École des Femmes* and Fielding, following him, in *Joseph Andrews,* say that comic and satiric "history" is a glass where "thousands in their closet" may see their own faces. Swift in his Preface to *The Battle of the Books* says just the opposite, that "Satyr is a sort of Glass, wherein Beholders do generally discover everybody's Face but their Own." Each of these views is of course correct.[12]

---

[12] This neither accepts nor rejects, though it does assert the critical irrelevance of, the classic apology made by the satirist or comic writer that his function is to ridicule and hence to correct vice or folly—*corriger les hommes en les divertissant.* The distinction confidently made by Meredith and others between satire and comedy, so much to the advantage of the latter, may or may not come in. And the critic may or may not believe—without special critical commitment in either case—that dunces and scoundrels were actually instructed or brought to repentance by the wit of Molière or Pope. It would seem that in some more or less primitive societies, satire has been thought to operate with a magically destructive force—

The laugh of self-enhancement in the presence of the comic figure must always have been in danger of being itself the occasion of laughter to the nearest spectator—but that spectator has often, happily, been the self. The German romantic theorists dwelt much in the region where subject and object are one. And laughter was one of their best avenues for getting there. The theory of laughter was reflexively subtilized by Jean Paul in his *Vorschule,* by Friedrich Schlegel, and by others into various shapes of self-criticism and sardonic transcendence. And after them comes Kierkegaard, in his double transcendence, by "irony" from the aesthetic to the ethical, and by "humor" from the ethical to the religious. "In order not to be distracted by the finite, by all the relativities in the world, the ethicist places the comical between himself and the world, thereby insuring himself against becoming comical through naive misunderstanding of his ethical passion." [13]

But a too close union between the laugher and his object may be one of the main dangers to which metaphysical laughing theory has been exposed. Laughter (because of its unreliable tendency to slide from the aloof to the sympathetic) is not a stern way of dealing with deviation. It is always somewhat too much like its object—undignified, frivolous, inferior. Hence it happened during the Renaissance that Aristotle himself was translated as

killing rats, raising blisters on faces, driving Lycambes and his daughter to hang themselves. (Cf. Robert C. Elliott, "The Satirist and Society," *A Journal of English Literary History,* xxi [September, 1954], 237–48.) Terror of ridicule may be one of the most permanent human passions. But it is presumably not the same as aesthetic experience.

[13] Søren Kierkegaard, *Concluding Unscientific Postscript,* trans. David F. Swenson (Princeton, 1944), p. 450.

saying that laughter is a form of baseness, a "fowling for the people's delight, or their fooling." And later on the romantic theorist in order to be superior had to be serious, looking at the comic in the light of the cosmic, and implicitly assigning to laughter a low place in his philosophy. "Reason does not joke," says Emerson in an essay on *The Comic,* "and men of reason do not."

> The essence of all jokes, of all comedy, seems to be an honest or well-intended halfness; . . . The balking of the intellect is comedy; and it announces itself physically in the pleasant spasms which we call laughter.

Pleasant spasms! "Peculiar explosions of laughter . . ." "Muscular irritation . . ." "Violent convulsions of the face and sides, and obstreperous roarings of the throat." [14] A note of patronage is clear. Another writer in English who leans toward the same predicament is Meredith, whose poems, if not his famous lecture on the "Comic Spirit," make a heavy linkage between laughter and the positivistic fetishes of nature, earth, brain, and blood. And here too, enjoying a high rank among sober laughers, appears Bergson, for whom the comic literary form reflects the limitation of its stereotyped and superficial objects, just as tragedy or serious art does the individuality and vitality of its own proper objects. Laughter is "a froth with a saline base. Like froth, it sparkles. It is gaiety itself. But the philosopher who

[14] Joseph Jones, "Emerson and Bergson on the Comic," *Comparative Literature,* I (Winter, 1949), 63–71, quoting Emerson's *Complete Works* (Centenary Edition), VIII, 158–173. Proper quotations could of course be made to yield the opposite emphasis. The perception of the comic "appears to be an essential element in a fine character."

gathers a handful to taste may find that the substance is scanty, and the aftertaste bitter." [15]

And so we have swung back once more, rather toward the embarrassments than toward the riches which laughter produces for the comic theorist and critic. And we have now to confess one more reason—or aspect of reasons already named—why the critic should, for the moment of his criticism at least, look askance at the pleasure of laughing. This is related less to any lofty dilemma than to just the need of criticism to keep to its object. The critic has not come before his audience to tell jokes, to demonstrate to them in any way at all that he knows how to make people laugh. It has been mainly when he has been bent on taking direct hold on laughter itself rather than on its objects that he has felt impelled to some such foredoomed attempt. The lugubriously heavy Germanic jokes, about Jews, about sex, and the like, which encumber Freud's pages will come to mind. Even Meredith, alert intellect that he is, may be felt to stumble when he challenges the national mentality and tries to persuade us, at some expense of words, about two incidents where the British would not laugh but *should,* and one where they would laugh but should *not.* Time and again [16] the writer on the comic should have had his warning. No matter how successful he is in other arenas as a wit, or perhaps all the more especially if he is a noted

[15] *Laughter, An Essay on the Meaning of the Comic,* trans. Cloudesley Brereton and Fred Rothwell (New York, 1928), p. 200.

[16] For a fairly recent instance, see Sir Alan Herbert, upon attempting a presidential address to the English Association upon the topic of the "English Laugh," greeted with pursed lips by an anonymous *TLS* arbiter (August 11, 1950, p. 501). "The trouble arises when the teacher uses his pointer . . . the sample joke assumes the wistfulness of a waning autumn light."

wit, he ought not to attempt the illustrated lecture. The general truth that there is no such thing as a scientific demonstration of the poetic is specially pointed up in the case of comedy by the sanction of laughter.

One of the main virtues of the six contributors to the present volume of essays on English stage comedy is that no one of them anywhere attempts to quote his materials in illustration of how funny they are. Mr. Barber's brief—and I believe inoffensive—allusion to laughter (p. 33) is a marked exception to the prevailing method of the volume. There is no implication, so far as I can see, in any of the essays that comedy should not or need not be funny. Yet a statement of the theses of our six authors (so far as their speculations admit being reduced to the simplicity of thesis) may sound severe enough: that Falstaff in the two parts of *Henry IV* is a character shaped on age-old lines of ritual meaning, a saturnalian king of misrule and then a scapegoat; that Shakespeare's final comedy *The Tempest* is a romanticized softening of certain Plautine lineaments of intrigue, the good old master, the clever willing servant, and the bungling oaf; that Ben Jonson's realistic comedies achieve their unity and meaning by organization around certain bizarre central symbols—the fanatically morose noise-hater, for instance, symbol of revulsion from the whole clattering business of metropolitan false living; that the after-gleams of English manners comedy, Sheridan and Wilde, are but pale affectations compared to the full social fire of Wycherley and Congreve; that the principle which makes Shaw's best comedies work, and which strives more or less ineffectually in his later comedies, is "Hegelian" dialectic; that

T. S. Eliot's comedies, somewhat like his Euripidean models, aim at a religious conversion of secular, even farcical materials, but that, unlike Euripides, Eliot scarcely succeeds. Here, one might say, are no laughing matters. The accent is scarcely that of the silvery laughter which Meredith partly manages to share with the Comic Spirit of his classic lecture. There is not even any of the somber-lurid funniness which exhales like a flickering gas-light along the ways of Bergson's metaphysical discussion, nor of the lumbering guffaw which may be heard heavily as from an inner chamber of the Freudian clinic. There are those who will point out quickly enough the prepared slant which the discussion has received from the Eliotic return to the quasi-tragic and quasi-religious melodramas of Euripides, from the dialectic habits of the conversational Shaw, even from the sandpapery rub of the didactic universe of Bartholomew Fair. There will undoubtedly be some who respond with indignation at the attempt to sublime Falstaff into anything so canonically primitive as a ritual scape-goat, and at the superior gaze turned by one of our authors upon the "good-natured sentimental dramas of comic intrigue" which Sheridan is said to have concocted for a "passive audience . . . bottle-fed on sermons."

All six of our essays are written in what may broadly be called the "classical" vein—as indeed every rebirth of English stage comedy has been in the classical vein. It was with a shrewd theo-retical insight, if not with complete theatrical success, that T. S. Eliot in a plan to return verse comedy to the English stage went back to the point in the history of Greek drama where Euripi-dean melodramatized tragedy was falling off into the patterns of tender emotion, intrigue, mistaken identity, foundling and

changeling plots from which the "New" Greek comedy, the
form prevailing on the stage ever since, was to take its cue. In
each new era the comic writer's talent has been to reinvent some
neglected formula. Herakles tippling and joking among the servants at the home of the bereft Admetus becomes, as Mr. Eliot
himself had to point out to his commentators, the unrevealed
psychiatrist at the ruined cocktail party of Edward Chamber-
layne—with a "Toory-ooly toory-iley, What's the matter with
One-Eyed Riley?" Prospero and Ariel reenact, in a strange new
context of island enchantments, the Plautine negotiations of the
benevolent master and crafty slave. Make the slave a willing but
subordinate and perhaps not brilliant charismatic personality, and
the master a patient, far-scheming, priestly psychiatrist, and you
have the interesting scene in Harcourt-Reilly's consulting room
at the start of Eliot's second act:

REILLY: It was necessary to delay his appointment
To lower his resistance. But what I mean is,
Does he trust your judgment?

ALEX: Yes, implicitly.
It's not that he regards me as very intelligent,
But he thinks I'm well informed: the sort of person
Who would know the right doctor, as well as the right shops.
Besides, he was ready to consult any doctor
Recommended by anyone except his wife.

REILLY: I had already impressed upon her
That she was not to mention my name to him.

ALEX: With your usual foresight.

But the essays which make up this volume are classical in a wider and deeper sense than that they are concerned with picking up such parallels, and indeed Mr. Arrowsmith on Eliot has not bothered that way at all. These essays are classical in the sense that they share the view which allows comic poetry and tragic poetry to be treated side by side in Aristotle's treatise on the *Art of Fiction.*[17] The implications of Aristotle's arrangement and of the Greek theatrical habit itself gradually shaded off into something different. As for comedy and satire, said Horace, we will inquire another time whether this kind of writing is really poetry or not. Of course he was joking, at least in part. But it has been along this line that later times, and especially our own, when laughter itself has become the object of a quasi-literary theoretical inquiry, have tended to assign comic theory its own special and inferior place, apart from serious poetics. Metaphysical wit and irony have been recent avenues of serious realliance with the laughing spirit of poetry. But to be yet more inclusive and venture a concern even for the comic (not as Emerson did it, not as Bergson, not quite perhaps even as Meredith, but in the manner of some new critic—more or less I think in the manner of our present six critics) may be the most urgent requirement for a progressive criticism of poetry today.

And lastly, there is another sense and a very important one in which the essays in this volume are classical. Though they are all interested more or less overtly in symbols, and though two of

[17] L. J. Potts once more, in a translation (*Aristotle on the Art of Fiction* [Cambridge, 1953]) which has the great merit of making Aristotle speak as if he knew what he meant—in a more or less continuous discourse.

them at least are in the full mythic and ritual mode, I believe that each of them keeps clear of that modern heresy which wants to make myth a new kind of canonical poetic subject matter or a guaranteed poetic idiom. As Jung at least (among the psychiatrists) will almost say,[18] there is a difference between a graceful and a clumsy "dream," a well-made and an ill-made "myth" or version of myth—between, let us say, a cliché myth and a real metaphoric utterance. This difference is specialized and written large in the world of poetry. At least two of our essays, the first and the last, are devoted to a formal insistence upon the critical significance of this kind of difference. It is through his recognizing and discussing this difference that the literary critic— whether of tragedy or of comedy—reveals that his expertise is not specifically that of the anthropologist and mythologue, but that of the literary critic.

[18] C. G. Jung, *Modern Man in Search of a Soul* (London, 1936), pp. 15, 79, 185, 194, 198.

C. L. Barber

◆§ FROM RITUAL TO COMEDY: AN EXAMINATION OF *HENRY IV*

My general concern is with the relation of comedy to analogous forms of symbolic action in folk rituals: not only the likenesses of comedy to ritual, but the differences, the features of comic form which make it comedy and not ritual. I want to point out what seem to me striking analogies between the comedy in the two parts of *Henry IV* and the customary misrule of traditional saturnalian holidays.[1] These analogies, I think, prove to be useful critical tools: they lead us to see structure in the play. And they also raise fascinating historical and theoretical questions about the relation of drama to other products of culture. One way in which our time has been seeing the universal in literature has been to find in complex literary works patterns which are analogous to myths and rituals and which can be regarded as archetypes, in some sense primitive or fundamental. I find this approach very exciting indeed. But at the same time, such analysis can be misleading if it leads to equating the literary form

[1] This paper is a development of an interpretation of *Henry IV* originally sketched in a more general article, "The Saturnalian Pattern in Shakespeare's Comedy," *Sewanee Review*, LIX (Autumn, 1951), 593–611. A number of sentences from the earlier account are included here in the course of setting up the problem of distinguishing comedy from ritual.

with primitive analogues. When we deal with so developed an art as Shakespeare's, in so complex an epoch as the Renaissance, primitive patterns may be seen in literature mainly because literary imagination, exploiting the heritage of literary form, disengages them from the suggestions of a complex culture. And the primitive levels are articulated in the course of reunderstanding their nature—indeed, the primitive can be fully expressed only on condition that the artist can deal with it in a most civilized way. Shakespeare presents patterns analogous to magic and ritual in the process of redefining magic as imagination, ritual as social action.

Shakespeare was neither primitive nor primitivistic, for in his culture what we search out and call primitive was in the blood and bone as a matter of course. The problem was to deal with it, to master it. The Renaissance was a moment when educated men were modifying a ceremonial conception of human life to create a historical conception. The ceremonial view, which assumed that names and meanings are fixed and final, expressed experience as pageant and ritual—pageant where the right names could march in proper order, or ritual where names could be changed in the right, the proper way. The historical view expresses life as drama. People in drama are not identical with their names, for they gain and lose their names, their status, and meaning—and not by settled ritual: the gaining and losing of names, of meaning, is beyond the control of any set ritual sequence. Shakespeare's plays are full of pageantry and of action patterned in a ritualistic way. But the pageants are regularly interrupted; the rituals are abortive or perverted; or if they succeed, they succeed against odds or in an unexpected fashion. The people in the plays try to organize their lives by pageant and ritual, but the plays are dramatic precisely because the effort fails. This failure drama presents as history and personality; in the largest perspective, as destiny. At the heart of the plays there is, I think, a fascination with the individualistic use or abuse of ritual—with magic.

There is an intoxication with the possibility of an omnipotence of mind by which words might become things, by which a man might wear divinity, might achieve, by making his own ritual, an unlimited power to incarnate meaning. This fascination is expressed in the poetry by which Shakespeare's people envisage their ideal selves. But his drama also expresses an equal and complementary awareness that magic is delusory, that words can become things or lead to deeds only within a social group, by virtue of a historical and psychological situation beyond the mind and discourse of any one man. This awareness of limitations is expressed by the ironies, whether comic or tragic, which Shakespeare embodies in the dramatic situations of his speakers, the ironies which bring down the selves or meanings which fly high in winged words.

We can explore one instance of this dramatic tension by looking in *Henry IV* at the relation of Shakespeare's festive comedy to ritual prototypes. As I see it, the gay comedy in Shakespeare is fundamentally saturnalian rather than satiric. A saturnalian pattern for organizing experience came to Shakespeare from many sources, in both social and artistic tradition. In the theatrical institution of clowning, the clown or Vice, when Shakespeare started to write, was a recognized anarchist who made aberration obvious by carrying release to absurd extremes. The cult of fools and folly, half social and half literary, embodied a similar polarization of experience. In social life, folly was customarily cultivated on traditional holidays such as Shrove Tuesday, Hocktide, May Day, Whitsuntide, Midsummer Eve, Harvest Home, and the twelve days of Christmas ending with Twelfth Night. The festival occasion provides a paradigm for the organization of impulse and awareness not only in those comedies where Shakespeare drew largely and directly on holiday motifs, like *Love's Labour's Lost, A Midsummer Night's Dream,* and *Twelfth Night,* but also in plays where there is relatively little direct use of holiday, notably *As You Like It* and *Henry IV.* The language that described festive occasions, or was used in them, provides a vocabulary for making explicit the "form of mirth" in the plays about pleasure. The attitudes adopted on holiday were archetypes in English Renaissance culture for the attitudes adopted about pleasure whenever people set out to have a good time. So Shakespeare's gay comedy dramatizes pleasure as release from normal limitations, and the judgments implicit in its humor primarily concern the relation between man and the nature celebrated by holiday, not relations between social classes or types. The plays give form to feeling and knowledge by a movement which can be summarized in the formula: *through release to clarification.*

I cannot even survey Shakespeare's development in relation to this holiday tradition here. My view, briefly, is that, although he began writing comedy with literary models (Plautus, Italian comedy, and narrative romances), he found a satisfactory form for the whole play only when, in *Love's Labour's Lost* and *A*

Midsummer Night's Dream, he shaped the whole action so as to express the release of a revel and so provide occasion for comic clarification of the relation between man's vital energies and the rest of his experience.

My thesis is that, in creating the Falstaff comedy, Shakespeare fused two main saturnalian traditions: the clowning customary on the stage, and the folly customary on holiday. Northrop Frye has effectively summarized the holiday aspect of Falstaff in saying that he is "a mock king, a lord of misrule, and his tavern is a saturnalia." [2] To see Falstaff in this role is not to suppose that Shakespeare arbitrarily imitates festivities at the Inns of Court or elsewhere, though such experience obviously is used. Rather, it seems to me, Shakespeare arrives at such a figure by developing the saturnalian implications of the clown's role in the directions suggested by the saturnalian customs and sensibility of his time and in response to the need for such a role within the imaginative economy of the whole complex historical drama which he was working out.

The tradition of clowning had been from long before Shakespeare integrally related to the use of double plots. William Empson has made some fine observations here, to which I am indebted.[3] It was of course a practice, going back at least as far as the *Second Shepherd's Play,* for the clowns to present a bur-

[2] "The Argument of Comedy," *English Institute Essays, 1948,* ed. by D. A. Robertson, Jr. (New York, 1949), p. 71. Mr. Frye's essay brilliantly summarizes Shakespeare's relation to the whole tradition of literary comedy. His account of the way comic form expresses reconciliation is a more generalized description than mine here; it outlines an "argument" which fits the saturnalian pole of comic release as well as the idyllic and millenial.

[3] Mr. Empson's discussion of the effects achieved by such double plots is in *English Pastoral Poetry* (New York, 1938), chap. ii.

lesque version of actions performed seriously by their betters. Wagner's conjuring in *Dr. Faustus* is an obvious example. In the drama just before Shakespeare began writing, there are a great many parallels of this sort between the low comedy and the main action. One suspects that they often resulted from the initiative of the clown performer—he was, as Sidney said, thrust in "by head and shoulders to play a part in majestical matters"— and the handiest part to play was a low take-off of what the high people were doing. Though Sidney objected that the procedure was "without decency or decorum," such burlesque, when properly controlled, had an artistic logic which Shakespeare was quick to develop.

At the simplest level the clowns were foils, as one of the aristocrats remarks in *Love's Labour's Lost:*

> 'Tis some policy
> To have one show worse than the king's and his company.

But burlesque could also have a positive effect, as a vehicle for expressing aberrant impulse and thought. When the aberration was made relevant to the main action, clowning could provide both release for impulses which run counter to decorum and the clarification about limits which comes from going beyond the limit. Shakespeare used this movement from release to clarification with masterful control in clown episodes as early as *Henry VI, Part II.* The scenes of the Jack Cade rebellion in that history are an astonishingly consistent expression of anarchy by clowning: the popular rising is presented throughout as a saturnalia, ignorantly undertaken in earnest; Cade's motto is "then are we in order when we are most out of order."

The implications of a saturnalian attitude are more drastically and complexly expressed in *Henry IV* than anywhere else, because here saturnalia is presented along with other kinds of experience, in an environment, so that Shakespeare dramatizes not only holiday but also the need for holiday and the need to limit holiday. Misrule is more drastic and meaningful here than in, say, *Twelfth Night,* because misrule is presented along with rule and along with the tensions that challenge rule. In the idyllic plays there is a humor of perspective which recognizes the limitations of the reigning festive moment by looking outward, from it, to the work-a-day world beyond. But in the two parts of *Henry IV,* holiday is balanced against everyday and doomsday within the play. The comedy expresses impulses and awareness excluded by the urgency and decorum of political life, so that the comic and serious strains are contrapuntal, each conveying ironies limiting the other.

The issue, so far as it concerns Prince Hal, can be summarized quite adequately in our key terms. As the nonhistorical material came to Shakespeare in *The Famous Victories of Henry the Fifth,* the prince was cast in the traditional role of the prodigal son while his disreputable companions functioned as tempters in the same general fashion as the Vice of the morality plays. At one level Shakespeare keeps this pattern, but he shifts the emphasis away from simple moral terms. The issue, in his hands, is not whether Hal will be good or bad but whether he will be noble or degenerate, whether his holiday will become his everyday. The interregnum of a Lord of Misrule, delightful in its moment, might develop into the anarchic reign of a favorite dominating a dissolute king. Hal's secret, which he confides early to the audi-

ence, is that for him Falstaff is merely a pastime, to be dismissed
in due course:

> If all the year were playing holidays,
> To sport would be as tedious as to work.

The prince's sports, accordingly, express not dissoluteness but
a fine excess of vitality—"as full of spirit as the month of May"
—together with a capacity for occasionally looking at the world
as though it were upside down. His energy is controlled by an
inclusive awareness of the rhythm in which he is living: despite
appearances, he will not make the mistake which undid Richard II,
who played at saturnalia until it caught up with him in earnest.
During the battle of Shrewsbury (when, in Hotspur's phrase,
"Doomsday is near"), Hal dismisses Falstaff with "What! is't a
time to jest and dally now?" This sense of timing, of the relation
of holiday to everyday, contributes to establishing the prince as
an inclusive, sovereign nature. At the close of battle, in the
moment of stillness when Hal stands poised above the prostrate
bodies of Hotspur and Falstaff, his position on the stage and
his lines about the two heroes express a nature which includes
within a larger order the now subordinated parts of life which
are represented in those two: in Hotspur, honor, the social obliga-
tion to courage and self-sacrifice, a value which has been isolated
in this magnificently anarchical feudal lord to become almost
the whole of life; and in Falstaff, the complementary *joie de vivre*
which rejects all social obligations because "I like not such grin-
ning honour as Sir Walter hath." At this point, Shakespeare was
in a wonderful position to end *Henry IV;* he could have left
Falstaff really dead, since he is effectually dead for the Prince.

Instead the dramatist brought him back to life, jumping up like Bottom after Pyramus in a triumph which reminds one of the comic resurrections in the St. George plays.

When Falstaff jumps up, his apology for counterfeiting cuts deeply indeed, because it does not apply merely to himself; we can relate it, as Empson has shown, to the counterfeiting of the king. Bolingbroke knows when it is time to counterfeit, both in this battle, where he survives because he has many marching in his coats, and throughout the political career where, as he acknowledges to Hal, he manipulates the symbols of majesty with a calculating concern for ulterior results. L. C. Knights, noticing this relation and the burlesque, elsewhere in Falstaff's part, of the attitudes of chivalry, concluded with nineteenth-century critics like Ulrici and Victor Hugo that the comedy should be taken as a devastating satire on war and government.[4] But this is obviously an impossible, anachronistic view, based on the assumption of the age of individualism that politics and war are unnatural activities that can be done without. Knights would have it that the audience should feel a jeering response when Henry sonorously declares, after Shrewsbury: "Thus ever did rebellion find rebuke." This interpretation makes a shambles of the heroic moments of the play—makes them clearly impossible to act. My own view, as my introductory remarks will have made clear, is that the dynamic relation of comedy and serious action is saturnalian rather than satiric, that the misrule works, through the whole dramatic rhythm, to consolidate rule. But it is also true, as Empson remarks, that "the double plot is carrying a fearful strain here."[5] Shakespeare is putting an enormous pressure on the

[4] "A Note on Comedy," *Determinations,* ed. by F. R. Leavis (London, 1934).
[5] *Some Versions of Pastoral* (London, 1935), p. 47.

comedy to resolve the challenge posed by the ironic perceptions presented in his serious action.

This can be made clearer, I hope, by reference now to the scapegoat aspect of saturnalian ritual. We do not need to assume that Shakespeare had any such ritual patterns consciously in mind; whatever his conscious intention, it seems to me that these analogues illuminate patterns which his poetic drama presents concretely and dramatically. After such figures as the Mardi Gras or Carnival have presided over a revel, they are frequently turned on by their followers, tried in some sort of court, convicted of sins notorious in the village during the last year, and burned or buried in effigy to signify a new start. In other ceremonies described in *The Golden Bough,* mockery kings appear as recognizable substitutes for real kings, stand trial in their stead, and carry away the evils of their realms into exile or death. One such scapegoat figure, as remote as could be from Shakespeare, is the Tibetan King of the Years, who enjoyed, until very recently at least, ten days' misrule during the annual holiday of Buddhist monks at Lhasa. At the climax of his ceremony, after doing what he liked while collecting bad luck by shaking a black yak's tail over the people, he mounted the temple steps and ridiculed the representative of the Grand Lama, proclaiming heresies like "What we perceive through the five senses is no illusion. All you teach is untrue." A few minutes later, discredited by a cast of loaded dice, he was chased off to exile and possible death in the mountains.[6] One cannot help thinking of Falstaff's catechism on honor, spoken just before another valuation of honor is expressed in the elevated blank verse of a hero confronting death: "Can honour . . . take away the grief of a

[6] See James G. Frazer, *The Scapegoat* (London, 1914), pp. 218–23.

wound? No. . . . What is honour? a word. What is that word, honour? Air." And Hal's final expulsion of Falstaff appears in the light of these analogies to carry out an impersonal pattern, not merely political but ritual in character. After the guilty reign of Bolingbroke, the prince is making a fresh start as the new king. At a level beneath the moral notions of a personal reform, we can see a nonlogical process of purification by sacrifice—the sacrifice of Falstaff. The career of the old king, a successful usurper whose conduct of affairs has been skeptical and opportunistic, has cast doubt on the validity of the whole conception of a divinely ordained and chivalrous kingship to which Shakespeare and his society were committed. And before Bolingbroke, Richard II had given occasion for doubts about the rituals of kingship in an opposite way, by trying to use them magically. Shakespeare had shown Richard assuming that the symbols of majesty should be absolutes, that the names of legitimate power should be transcendently effective regardless of social forces. Now both these attitudes have been projected also in Falstaff; he carries to comically delightful and degraded extremes both a magical use of moral sanctions and the complementary opportunistic manipulation and skepticism. So the ritual analogy suggests that by turning on Falstaff as a scapegoat, as the villagers turned on their Mardi Gras, the prince can free himself from the sins, the "bad luck," of Richard's reign and of his father's reign, to become a king in whom chivalry and a sense of divine ordination are restored.

Now this process of carrying off bad luck, if it is to be made *dramatically* cogent, as a symbolic action accomplished in and by dramatic form, cannot take place magically in Shakespeare's play: the magical analogy can be only a useful way of organizing our awareness of a complex symbolic action. The expulsion of evil works as dramatic form only in so far as it is realized in a movement from participation to rejection which happens, moment by moment, in our response to Falstaff's clowning misrule. We watch Falstaff adopt one posture after another, in the effort to give himself meaning at no cost; and moment by moment we see that the meaning is specious. So our participation is repeatedly diverted to laughter. The laughter signalizes our mastery by understanding of the tendency which has been misapplied or carried to an extreme; this mastery leaves us free to laugh off energy originally mobilized to respond to a valid meaning.

Consider, for example, the use of magical notions of royal power in the most famous of all Falstaff's burlesques:

> By the Lord, I knew ye as well as he that made ye. . . .
> was it for me to kill the heir-apparent? Should I turn upon
> the true prince? Why, thou knowest I am as valiant as Her-
> cules; but beware instinct; the lion will not touch the true
> prince. Instinct is a great matter, I was a coward on instinct.
> I shall think the better of myself and thee during my life; I
> for a valiant lion, and thou for a true prince. But, by the Lord,
> lads, I am glad you have the money. Hostess, clap to the
> doors: watch to-night, pray to-morrow.

Here Falstaff has recourse to the brave conception that legitimate kingship has a magical potency. This is the sort of absolutist appeal to sanctions which Richard II keeps falling back on in his desperate "conjuration" by hyperbole:

> So when this thief, this traitor, Bolingbroke
>   . . . . .
> Shall see us rising in our throne, the east,
> His treasons will sit blushing in his face,
> Not able to endure the sight of day. . . .
>
> The breath of worldly men cannot depose
> The deputy elected by the Lord.
> For every man that Bolingbroke hath press'd
> To lift shrewd steel against our golden crown,
> God for his Richard hath in heavenly pay
> A glorious angel.

In Richard's case, a tragic irony enforces the fact that heavenly angels are of no avail if one's coffers are empty and the Welsh army have dispersed. In Falstaff's case, the irony is comically obvious, the "lies are like the father that begets them; gross as a mountain, open, palpable." Hal stands for the judgment side of our response, while Falstaff embodies the enthusiastic, irre-pressible conviction of fantasy's omnipotence. The Prince keeps returning to Falstaff's bogus "instinct": "Now, sirs . . . you are lions too, you ran away upon instinct, you will not touch the true prince; no, fie!" After enjoying the experience of seeing through such notions of magical majesty, he is never apt to make the mistake of assuming that, just because he is king, lions like Northumberland will not touch him. King Richard's bad luck came precisely from such an assumption—unexamined, of course, as fatal assumptions always are. Freud's account of bad luck, in *The Psychopathology of Everyday Life,* sees it as the expression of unconscious motives which resist the conscious goals of the personality. This view helps to explain how the acting out of disruptive motives in saturnalia or in comedy can serve to master potential aberration by revaluing it in relation to the whole of experience. So Falstaff, in acting out this absolutist aberration, is taking away what might have been Hal's bad luck, taking it away in a real, though not magical way: the comedy is a civilized equivalent of the primitive rite. I hope it will be clear by analogy that a similar mastery of potential aberration is promoted by the experience of seeing through Falstaff's burlesque of the sort of headlong chivalry presented seriously in Hotspur.

In order to put the symbolic action of the comedy in larger perspective, it will be worth while to consider further, for a moment, the relation of language to stage action and dramatic situation in *Richard II*. That play is a pioneering exploration of the semantics of royalty, shot through with talk about the potency and impotence of language. In the first part, we see a Richard who is possessor of an apparently magical omnipotence: for example, when he commutes Bolingbroke's banishment from ten to six years, Bolingbroke exclaims:

> How long a time lies in one little word!
> Four lagging winters and four wanton springs
> End in a word: such is the breath of kings.

Richard assumes he has such magic breath inevitably, regardless of the breath of worldly men. When he shouts things like "Is not the king's name twenty thousand names? Arm, arm, my name!" he carries the absolutist assumption to the giddiest verge of absurdity. When we analyze the magical substitution of words

for things in such lines, looking at them from outside the
rhythm of feeling in which they occur, it seems scarcely plausible
that a drama should be built around the impulse to adopt such
an assumption. It seems especially implausible in our own age,
when we are so conscious, on an abstract level, of the dependence
of verbal efficacy on the social group. The analytical situation
involves a misleading perspective, however; for, whatever your
assumptions about semantics, when you have to act, to be somebody or become somebody, there is a moment when you have
to have faith that the unknown world beyond will respond to
the names you commit yourself to as right names.[7] The Elizabethan mind, moreover, generally assumed that one played one's
part in a divinely ordained pageant where each man *was* his
name and the role his name implied. The expression of this faith,
and of the outrage of it, is particularly drastic in the Elizabethan
drama, which can be regarded, from this vantage, as an art form
developed to express the shock and exhilaration of the discovery
that life is not pageantry. As Professor Tillyard has pointed out,
Richard II is the most ceremonial of all Shakespeare's plays, and
the ceremony all comes to nothing.[8] In Richard's deposition
scene, one way in which anguish at his fall is expressed is by a
focus on his loss of names: he responds to Northumberland's "My
Lord—" by flinging out

> No lord of thine, thou haught insulting man,
> Nor no man's lord; I have no name, no title,

[7] I am indebted to my colleagues Professor Theodore Baird and Professor
G. Armour Craig for this general conception of the relations of names to developing
situations.

[8] See *Shakespeare's History Plays* (New York, 1946), pp. 245 ff.

> No, not that name was given me at the font,
> But 'tis usurp'd: alack the heavy day!
> That I have worn so many winters out,
> And know not now what name to call myself.
> O! that I were a mockery king of snow,
> Standing before the sun of Bolingbroke,
> To melt myself away in water-drops.

His next move is to call for the looking glass in which he stares at his face to look for the meaning the face has lost. To lose one's meaning, one's social role, is to be reduced to mere body.

Here again the tragedy can be used to illuminate the comedy. Since the Elizabethan drama was a double medium of words and of physical gestures, it frequently expressed the pathos of the loss of meaning by emphasizing moments when word and gesture, name and body, no longer go together, just as it presented the excitement of a gain of meaning by showing a body seizing on names when a hero creates his identity. In the deposition scene, Richard says "mark me how I will undo myself." Then he gives away by physical gestures the symbolic meanings which have constituted that self. When at last he has no name, the anguish is that the face, the body, remain when the meaning is gone. Of course there is also a narcissism in Richard's lines which, beneath the surface of his self-pity, relishes such reduction to his body, a self-love which looks towards fulfillment in that final reduction of all to the body which is death. This narcissistic need for the physical is the other side of the attitude that the magic of the crown should altogether transcend the physical—and the human:

Cover your heads, and mock not flesh and blood
With solemn reverence: throw away respect,
Tradition, form, and ceremonious duty,
For you have but mistook me all this while:
I live with bread like you, feel want,
Taste grief, need friends: subjected thus,
How can you say to me I am a king?

In expressing the disappointment of Richard's magical expectations, as well as their sweeping magnificence, the lines make
manifest the aberration which is mastered in the play by tragic
form.

The same sort of impulse is expressed and mastered by comic
form in the *Henry IV* comedy. When Richard wishes he were
a mockery king of snow, to melt before the sun of Bolingbroke,
the image expresses on one side the wish to escape from the
body with which he is left when his meaning has gone—to
weep himself away in water drops. But the lines also look wist-
fully towards games of mock royalty where, since the whole
thing is based on snow, the collapse of meaning need not hurt.
Falstaff is such a mockery king. To be sure, he is flesh and
blood, of a kind: he is tallow, anyway. He "sweats to death
And lards the lean earth as he walks along." (The image is
strikingly reminiscent of Richard's melting snowman.) Of course
he is not just a mockery, not just his role, not just bombast.
Shakespeare, as always, makes the symbolic role the product of
a life which includes contradictions of it, such as the morning-
after regrets when Falstaff thinks of the inside of a church and

notices that his skin hangs about him like an old lady's loose
gown. Falstaff is human enough so that "Were't not for laughing, . . . [we] should pity him." But we do laugh, because when
Falstaff's meanings collapse, almost nothing but make-believe has
been lost.

> PRINCE: Do thou stand for my father, and examine me
> upon the particulars of my life.
> FALSTAFF: Shall I? content: this chair shall be my state, this
> dagger my sceptre, and this cushion my crown.
> PRINCE: Thy state is taken for a joint-stool, thy golden
> sceptre for a leaden dagger, and thy precious rich crown for
> a pitiful bald crown!

Falstaff's effort to make his body and furnishings mean sovereignty is doomed from the start; he must work with a leaden
dagger, the equivalent of a Vice's dagger of lath. But Falstaff
does have golden words, and an inexhaustible vitality in using
them. He can name himself nobly, reordering the world verbally
so as to do himself credit:

> No, good my lord; banish Peto, banish Bardolph, banish
> Poins; but for sweet Jack Falstaff, kind Jack Falstaff, true
> Jack Falstaff, valiant Jack Falstaff, and therefore more valiant
> being, as he is, old Jack Falstaff, banish not him thy Harry's
> company: banish not him thy Harry's company: Banish
> plump Jack, and banish all the world.

I quote such familiar lines to recall their effect of incantation:
they embody an effort at a kind of magical naming. Each repe-

tition of "sweet Jack Falstaff, kind Jack Falstaff" aggrandizes an identity which the serial clauses caress and cherish. At the very end, in "plump Jack," the disreputable belly is glorified.

In valid heroic and majestic action, the bodies of the personages are constantly being elevated by becoming the vehicles of social meanings; in the comedy, such elevation becomes burlesque, and by the repeated failures to achieve a fusion of body and symbol, abstract meanings keep falling back into the physical. "A plague of sighing and grief! it blows a man up like a bladder." The repetition of such joking about Falstaff's belly makes it meaningful in a very special way, as a symbol of the process of inflation and reduction. So it represents the power of the individual life to continue despite the collapse of social roles. This continuing on beyond definitions is after all what we call "the body" in one main meaning of the term: Falstaff's belly is thus the essence of body —an essence which can be defined only dynamically, by failures of meaning. The effect of indestructible vitality is reinforced by the association of Falstaff's figure with the gay eating and drinking of Shrove Tuesday and Carnival. Whereas, in the tragedy, the reduction is to a body which can only die, here reduction is to a body which typifies our power to eat and drink our way through a shambles of intellectual and moral contradictions.

So we cannot resist sharing Falstaff's genial self-love when he commends his vision of plump Jack to the Prince, just as we share the ingenuous self-love of a little child. But the dramatist is ever on the alert to enforce the ironies that dog the tendency of fantasy to equate the self with "all the world." So a most monstrous watch comes beating at the doors which have been clapped to against care; everyday breaks in on holiday.

Part I can be summarized, in terms of our analogy, as the reign of Carnival; *Part II* as his trial. To put Carnival on trial, run him out of town, and burn or bury him is in folk custom a way of limiting, by ritual, the attitudes and impulses set loose by ritual. Such a trial, though conducted no doubt with gay hoots and jeers, serves to swing the mind round to a new vantage, where it sees misrule no longer as a benign release for the individual, but as a source of destructive consequences for society. This sort of reckoning is what *Part II* brings to Falstaff.

But Falstaff proves extremely difficult to bring to book—more difficult than an ordinary mummery king—because his burlesque and mockery are developed to a point where the mood of a moment crystallizes as a settled attitude of skepticism. In a static, monolithic society, a Lord of Misrule can be put back in his place after the revel with relative ease. The festive burlesque of solemn sanctities does not seriously threaten social values in a monolithic culture, because the license depends utterly upon what it mocks: liberty is unable to envisage any alternative to the accepted order except the standing of it on its head. But Shakespeare's culture was not monolithic: though its moralists assumed a single order, skepticism was beginning to have ground to stand on and look about—especially in and around London. So a Lord of Misrule figure, brought up, so to speak, from the country to the city, or from the traditional past into the changing present, could become on the Bankside the mouthpiece not merely for the dependent holiday skepticism which is endemic in a traditional society, but also for a dangerously self-sufficient everyday skepticism. When such a figure is set in an environment of sober-blooded great men behaving as opportunistically as he, the effect is to raise radical questions about social sanctities. At the end of *Part II,* the expulsion of Falstaff is presented by the dramatist as getting rid of this threat; he has recourse to a primitive procedure to meet a modern challenge. We shall find reason to question whether this use of ritual succeeds.

But the main body of *Part II,* what I am seeing as the trial as against the execution, is of course wonderfully effective drama. The first step in trying Carnival, the first step in ceasing to be his subjects, would be to stop calling him "My Lord" and call him instead by his right name, Misrule. Now this is just the step which Falstaff himself takes for us at the outset of *Part II;* when we first see him, he is setting himself up as an institution, congratulating himself on his powers *as* buffoon and wit. He glories in his role with what Dover Wilson has aptly called "comic hubris." [9] In the saturnalian scenes of *Part I,* where we first see him, it is impossible to say just who he is, for he is constantly renaming himself:

> . . . let not us that are squires of the night's body be called thieves of the day's beauty: let us be Diana's foresters, gentlemen of the shade, minions of the moon; and let men say, we be men of good government. . . .

Here Misrule is asking to be called Good Government, as it is his nature to do—though of course he does so with a wink which sets real good government at naught. But in *Part II,* Falstaff sets himself up at the outset as Falstaff:

[9] *The Fortunes of Falstaff* (New York, 1944), chap. v, "Falstaff High on Fortune's Wheel."

I am not only witty in myself, but the cause that wit is in other men.

                    .   .   .   .   .

A pox of this gout! or, a gout of this pox! for the one or the other plays the rogue with my great toe. 'Tis no matter if I do halt; I have the wars for my colour, and my pension shall seem the more reasonable. A good wit will make use of anything; I will turn diseases to commodity.

In the early portion of *Part I* he never spoke in asides, but now he constantly confides his schemes and his sense of himself to the audience. We do not have to see through him, but watch instead from inside his façades as he imposes them on others. Instead of warm amplifications centered on himself, his talk now consists chiefly of bland impudence or dry, denigrating comments on the way of the world. Much of the comedy is an almost Jonsonian spectacle where we relish a witty knave gulling fools.

It is this self-conscious Falstaff, confident of setting up his holiday license on an everyday basis, who at once encounters, of all awkward people, the Lord Chief Justice. From there on, during the first two acts, he is constantly put in the position of answering his way of life; in effect he is repeatedly called to trial and keeps eluding it only by a "more than impudent sauciness" and the privilege of his official employment in the wars. Mistress Quickly's attempt to arrest him is wonderfully ineffectual; but he notably fails to thrust the Lord Chief Justice from a level consideration. Hal and Poins then disguise themselves, not this

time for the sake of the incomprehensible lies that Falstaff will
tell, but in order to try him, to see him "bestow himself . . . in
his true colours." So during the first two acts we are repeatedly
put in the position of judging him, although we continue to
laugh with him. A vantage is thus established from which we
watch him in action in Gloucestershire, where the Justice he has
to deal with is so shallow that Falstaff's progress is a triumph.
The comedy is still delightful; Falstaff is still the greatest of
wits; but we are constantly shown that fun involves fraud.
Falstaff himself tells us so, with proud relish. Towards the end of
the play, Hal's reconciliation with his father and then with the
Lord Chief Justice reemphasizes the detached vantage of judgment. So no leading remarks are necessary to assure our noting
and marking when we hear Falstaff shouting, "Let us take any
man's horses; the laws of England are at my commandment.
Happy are they which have been my friends, and woe unto my
lord chief justice!" The next moment we watch Doll and the
Hostess being hauled off by beadles because "the man is dead
that you and Pistol beat among you."

Many of the basic structures in this action no doubt were
shaped by morality-play encounters between Virtues and Vices,
encounters which from our vantage today can be seen as part of
the festive and scapegoat pattern. The trial of Falstaff is so effective *as drama* because no one conducts it—it happens. Falstaff,
being a dramatic character, not a mummery, does not know
when he has had his day. And he does not even recognize the
authority who will finally sentence him: he mistakes Hal for a
bastard son of the king's. The result of the trial is to make us see

perfectly the necessity for the rejection of Falstaff as a man, as a favorite for a king, as the leader of an interest at court.

But, in justifying the rejection of Falstaff as a mode of aware-ness, I do not think that the dramatist is equally successful. The problem is not in justifying rejection morally but in making the process cogent *dramatically,* as in *Part I* we reject magical majesty or intransigent chivalry. The bad luck which in *Part II* Falstaff goes about collecting, by shaking the black yak's tail of his wit over people's heads, is the impulse to assume that nothing is sacred. In a play concerned with ruthless political maneuver, much of it conducted by impersonal state functionaries, Falstaff turns up as a functionary too, with his own version of maneuver and impersonality: "If the young dace be a bait for the old pike, I see no reason in the law of nature but I may snap at him." Now this attitude is a most appropriate response to the behavior of the high factions beneath whose struggles Falstaff plies his retail trade. In the Gaultree parleys, Lord John rebukes the Archbishop for his use of the counterfeited zeal of God—and then himself uses a counterfeited zeal of gentlemanly friendship to trick the rebels into disbanding their forces. The difference between his behavior and Falstaff's is of course that Lancaster has the sanc-tion of the state on his side, a sanction supported, if not by legitimacy, at least by the desperate need for social order. This is a real difference, but a bare and harsh one. After all, Falstaff's little commonwealth of man has its pragmatic needs too: as he explains blandly to the Justice, he needs great infamy, because "he that buckles him in my belt cannot live in less."

The trouble with trying to get rid of this attitude merely by getting rid of Falstaff is that the attitude is too pervasive in the whole society of the play, whether public or private. It is too obviously *not* just a saturnalian mood, an extravagant aberration; it is presented instead as in grain, as the way of the world. Shakespeare might have let the play end with this attitude dominant, a harsh recognition that life is a nasty business where the big fishes eat the little fishes, with the single redeeming consideration that political order is better than anarchy, so that there is a pragmatic virtue in loyalty to the power of the state. But instead the dramatist undertakes, in the last part of the play, to expel this view of the world and to dramatize the creation of legitimacy and sanctified social power. Although the final scenes are fascinating, with all sorts of illuminations, it seems to me that at this level they partly fail.

We have seen that Shakespeare typically uses ritual patterns of behavior and thought precisely in the course of making clear, by tragic or comic irony, that rituals have no *magical* efficacy. The reason for his failure at the close of *Part II* is that at this point he uses ritual, not ironically transformed into drama, but magically. To do this involves a restriction instead of an extension of awareness. An extension of control and awareness is consummated in the epiphany of Hal's majesty while he is standing over Hotspur and Falstaff at the end of *Part I*. But *Part II* ends with a drastic restriction of awareness which goes with the embracing of magical modes of thought, not humorously but sentimentally.

It is true that the latter half of *Part II* very effectively builds up to this finale by recurrent expression of a laboring need to be rid of a growth or humor. King Henry talks of the body of his kingdom as foul with rank diseases, and recalls Richard's prophecy that "foul sin gathering head Shall break into corruption." There are a number of other images of expulsion, of which I can notice here only the very striking case where the rebels speak of the need to "purge the obstructions which begin to stop Our very veins of life." Henry himself, of course, is sick in the last half of the play, and there are repeated suggestions that his sickness is the consequence both of his sinful usurpation and of the struggle to defend it. Since his usurpation was almost a public duty, and his defense of order clearly for England's sake as well as his own advantage, he becomes in these last scenes almost a sacrificial figure, a king who sins for the sake of society, suffers for society in suffering for his sin, and carries his sin off into death. Hal speaks of the crown having "fed upon the body of my father." Henry, in his last long speech, summarizes this pattern in saying:

> God knows, my son,
> By what by-paths and indirect crook'd ways
> I met this crown; and I myself know well
> How troublesome it sat upon my head:
> To thee it shall descend with better quiet,
> Better opinion, better confirmation;
> For all the soil of the achievement goes
> With me into the earth.

The same image of burying sin occurs in some curious lines with which Hal reassures his brothers:

> My father is gone wild into his grave,
> For in his tomb lie my affections.

This conceit not only suggests an expulsion of evil, but hints
at the patricidal motive which is referred to explicitly elsewhere
in these final scenes and is the complement of the father-son
atonement.

Now this sacrificial imagery, where used by and about the old
king, is effectively dramatic, because it does not ask the audience to abandon any part of the awareness of the human, social
situation which the play as a whole has expressed. But the case
is altered when Hal turns on "that father ruffian" Falstaff. The
new king's whip-lash lines stress Falstaff's age and glance at his
death:

> I know thee not, old man: fall to thy prayers;
> How ill white hairs become a fool and jester!
> I have long dream'd of such a kind of man,
> So surfeit-swell'd, so old, and so profane;
> But being awak'd, I do despise my dream.
> Make less thy body hence, and more thy grace;
> Leave gormandising; know the grave doth gape
> For thee thrice wider than for other men.

The priggish tone, to which so many readers, including Bradley,
have objected, can be explained at one level as appropriate to the
solemn occasion of a coronation. But it goes with a drastic narrow-
ing of awareness. There are of course occasions in life when
people close off parts of their minds—a coronation is a case in
point: Shakespeare, it can be argued, is simply putting such an
occasion into his play. But even his genius could not get around
the fact that to block off awareness of irony is contradictory to
the very nature of drama, which has as one of its functions the
extension of such awareness. Hal's lines, redefining his holiday

with Falstaff as a dream, and then despising the dream, seek to invalidate that holiday pole of life, instead of including it, as his lines on his old acquaintance did at the end of *Part I*. Elsewhere in Shakespeare, to dismiss dreams categorically is foolhardy. And those lines about the thrice-wide grave: are they a threat or a joke? We cannot tell, because the sort of awareness that would confirm a joke is being damped out: "Reply not to me with a fool-born jest." If ironies about Hal were expressed by the context, we could take the scene as the representation of his becoming a prig. But there is simply a blur in the tone, a blur which results, I think, from a retreat into magic by the *dramatist,* as distinct from his characters. Magically, the line about burying the belly is exactly the appropriate threat. It goes with the other images of burying sin and wildness and conveys the idea that the grave can swallow what Falstaff's belly stands for. To assume that one can cope with a pervasive attitude of mind by dealing physically with its most prominent symbol—what is this but magic-mongering? It is the same sort of juggling which we get in Henry IV's sentimental lines taking literally the name of the Jerusalem chamber in the palace:

> Laud be to God! Even there my life must end.
> It hath been prophesied to me many years
> I should not die but in Jerusalem.

One can imagine making a mockery of Henry's pious ejaculation by catcalling a version of his final lines at the close of *Richard II:*

> Is this that voyage to the Holy Land
> To wash the blood from off your guilty hand?

An inhibition of irony goes here with Henry's making the symbol do for the thing, just as it does with Hal's expulsion of Falstaff. A return to an official view of the sanctity of state is achieved by sentimental use of magical relations.

Henry IV is only one instance, but we can now at least suggest a few tentative conclusions of a general sort about the relation of comedy to ritual. It appears from this example that comedy uses ritual in the process of redefining ritual as the expression of particular personalities in particular circumstances. The heritage of ritual gives universality and depth. The persons of the drama make the customary gestures developed in ritual observance, and, in doing so, they project in a wholehearted way attitudes which are not normally articulated at large. At the same time, the dramatization of such gestures involves being aware of their relation to the whole of experience in a way which is not necessary for the celebrants of a ritual proper. In the actual observance of customary misrule, the control of the disruptive motives which the festivity expresses is achieved by the group's recognition of the place of the whole business within the larger rhythm of their continuing social life. No one need decide, therefore, whether the identifications involved in the ceremony are magically valid or merely expressive. But in the drama, perspective and control depend on presenting, along with the ritual gestures, an expression of a social situation out of which they grow. So the drama controls magic by reunderstanding it as imagination: dramatic irony constantly dogs the wish that the mock king be real, that the self be all the world or set all the world at naught. When, through a failure of irony, the dramatist presents ritual as magically valid, the result is sentimental, since drama lacks the kind of control which comes when the auditors are participants. Sentimental "drama," that which succeeds in being neither comedy nor tragedy, can be regarded from this vantage as theater used as a substitute for ritual, without the commitment to participation proper to ritual nor the commitment to the fullest understanding proper to comedy or tragedy.

Historically, Shakespeare's drama can be seen as part of the process by which our culture has moved from absolutist modes of thought towards a historical and psychological view of man by which all the world is a stage. But though the Renaissance moment made the tension between a magical and an empirical view of man particularly acute, this pull is of course always present: it is the tension between the heart and the world. By incarnating ritual as plot and character, the dramatist finds an embodiment for the heart's drastic gestures while recognizing how the world keeps comically and tragically giving them the lie.

◄§ *THE TEMPEST* AND THE ANCIENT COMIC TRADITION

In *The Tempest* Shakespeare abandons the three familiar *milieux* in which most of his plays are set (classical antiquity, medieval England, and Renaissance Europe) [1] for a nameless island which is remote even from that Tunis which is itself, according to Antonio, "ten leagues beyond man's life." This island is not only uncharted, it is one on which anything can happen; "All torment, trouble, wonder, and amazement Inhabits heere." The poet places his characters in a world which seems to be purely of his own creating; it seems in this respect significant that, in spite of prodigies of *Quellenforschung,* no satisfactory source of *The Tempest* has yet been identified.

In the so-called "romances" of Shakespeare's last period there is an accelerated flight from probability; it is a movement beyond the "probable impossibility" to the complete impossibility. In *The Tempest* the laws which govern objects existing in space and time as we know them are imperiously suspended. Until the solemn moment when Prospero abjures his rough magic, the action develops in a world which defies nature: "These are not naturall evens, they strengthen From strange, to stranger." One

---

[1] Cf. Gilbert Highet, *The Classical Tradition* (Oxford, 1949), p. 194.

wonders how Prospero can keep his promise to the bewildered Alonso—"I'le resolve you (Which to you shall seeme probable) of every These happend accidents."

A recent production by the Yale Dramatic Association presented *The Tempest* as "science-fiction"; the shipwreck scene took place in a space ship, and the action which takes place away from Prospero's cell was seen on a gigantic television screen, tuned in by a Prospero who sat before a control board which buzzed and flashed green light. The point was well taken: Shakespeare has in fact done what the modern science-fictioneers do—substituted for the normal laws of the operation of matter a new set of laws invented for the occasion.

Such a substitution creates great possibilities for what Aristotle called "Spectacle," and if the Yale Dramatic Association developed those possibilities somewhat exuberantly along modern lines they at least did no worse than Dryden and Davenant in 1667, whose stage direction for Act I, scene 1, reads, in part: "This Tempest . . . has many dreadful Objects in it, as several Spirits in horrid shapes flying down among the Sailers, then rising and crossing in the Air. And when the Ship is sinking, the whole House is darken'd, and a shower of Fire falls upon 'em."

But novel and fantastic effects (and in this play it is clear that Shakespeare was interested in producing them) have their dangerous side; they may, by trading too much on it, destroy that willing suspension of disbelief on which every dramatic performance depends—the audience may come to feel, with Gonzalo, "Whether this be Or be not, I'le not sweare." The dramatist by asking too much, may lose everything. Such a defiance of the normal laws of cause and effect in the operations of nature is especially dangerous in comedy, for comedy's appeal, no matter how contrived the plot may be, is to the audience's sense of solid values in a real world, to a critical faculty which can recognize the inappropriate. Tragedy, which questions normal human assumptions, may introduce the super- and the hypernatural more safely than comedy, which depends on the solidity of those assumptions for a response. A comic poet who sets his characters in action, not in the world as we know it but in one which defies our expectation, must compensate for the strangeness of the events by making the essences and relationships of the characters immediately and strikingly familiar. To put it another way, the fantasy and originality of the setting must be balanced and disciplined by a rigid adherence to tradition in character and plot.

This, I suggest, is a valid formula for *The Tempest*. It has certainly the most extraordinary and fantastic setting, for the sorcery of Prospero is a stranger thing than the familiar English fairy magic of *The Midsummer Night's Dream*. But in other ways it is the most rigidly traditional of all Shakespeare's comedies—with one exception. The exception is *The Comedy of Errors,* which is however apprentice-work, a typical Renaissance *remaniement* of a Plautine original. *The Tempest* is as original as *The Comedy of Errors* is imitative; and yet they are the beginning and end of the same road. For the traditional foundation on which *The Tempest*'s cloud-capped towers are raised is the ancient comedy of Plautus, Terence, and (though the name would not have meant much to Shakespeare) Menander.

Like all proper foundations, this one is not conspicuous. But

there are odd corners where its outline is visible in the super-
structure. This, for example:

> PROSPERO (*to Ariel*): She did confine thee
> By helpe of her more potent Ministers,
> And in her most unmittigable rage,
> Into a cloven Pyne, within which rift,
> Imprison'd, thou didst painefully remaine
> A dozen yeeres: within which space she di'd,
> And left thee there: where thou didst vent thy groanes
> As fast as Mill-wheeles strike.

The groans of a disobedient spirit imprisoned in a cloven
pine by a "blew ey'd hag" come "as fast as Mill-wheeles strike":
the simile illustrates the unfamiliar by appeal to an aspect of
ordinary experience. Yet not, presumably, Ariel's ordinary experience: there are no mills in the strange economy of Prospero's
island. The simile illustrates by an appeal from one world to
another, with an anachronism the reverse of those Homeric
similes which compare conditions of the heroic age to those of the
poet's own time. (Homer compares the voice of Achilles to a
trumpet, an instrument which the embattled heroes of his poem
never mention or use, almost certainly because it had not yet
been invented.) The mill wheels of Shakespeare's simile come
not from his own world but from the world of Plautine comedy,
where with monotonous frequency the rebellious slave is threatened or actually punished with an assignment to the brutal labor
of the mill. And in this fantastic context, where Ariel ("my
slave, as thou reportst thyselfe") is reminded of his punishment
for former disobedience and threatened with even worse punish-

ment for present disobedience, the simile gives a touch of familiarity and proportion to the outlandish details of Ariel's nature and status.

Here the classical precedent is for a moment distinctly visible, but in general it does its work the more efficiently because it is not obtrusive. Below the strange and brilliant surface composed of medieval magic and Renaissance travel tales, the initial situation, the nature and relationships of most of the characters, the development of the action and its final solution are all conjugations of the basic paradigms of classical comedy.

One of the most influential of these paradigms relates to the existence in ancient society of a dividing line stricter and more difficult to cross than any social barrier has been since: the distinction between slave and free. The free man could not imagine a misfortune worse than slavery, nor the slave a greater blessing than freedom. Slave and free were not so much separate classes as separate worlds: Aristotle could go so far as to claim that they were separate natures. This division was the most important sociological datum of ancient society, affecting men's attitude toward each other with a power almost as great as that of natural differences of sex or color. Among other things it provided a fixed contrast of condition and standards on which comedy could be based.

Ancient tragedy at the height of its development ignores the division and deals only with free men; Attic tragedy did not deal with slaves until Euripides introduced them, and this innovation was one of the main grounds for the conservative attack on him. The place for slaves was comedy, which, says Aristotle, "is an imitation of characters of a lower type"; and the lowest type imaginable was the slave. Comic slaves could be beaten, could curse, lie, cheat, be drunken, lecherous, and cowardly to the limit of the free audience's capacity for laughter without offending its sense of propriety and human dignity. Such an exhibition might in fact be considered to have a moral effect; in Plutarch's Life of Lycurgus (ch. 28) we are told that at Sparta the ephors introduced into the military dining-halls Helots who had been deliberately inebriated as a spectacle to teach the young what drunkenness was like; they also made the Helots learn songs and dances that were, to quote Plutarch again, "ignoble and ridiculous."

This was of course, not a real dramatic performance (though there is evidence of some kind of comic performance at Sparta from quite early times); at Athens the picture is clearer. It is perhaps only a coincidence that the chorus of satyrs in the only two surviving specimens of the humorous satyr play are, in the plot of the plays, temporarily enslaved, but it is evident that typical Athenian Old Comedy depended heavily on the laughter to be extracted from the low proclivities and activities of slaves. Aristophanes is not typical, but he indicates what is typical in a famous passage of self-congratulation with sets forth his claim to have ennobled comedy. Among other things he claims to have "liberated the slaves, whom the poets always brought on stage howling, all for the sake of the same old joke, so that a fellow-slave could make fun of their stripes, and ask them, 'What happened to your hide, poor devils? Were your sides assaulted by a whiplash army that cut down the trees on your back?'" Aristophanes did not, of course, dispense entirely with servile humor, rather he seems to have adapted it to subtler purposes by introducing witty contrasts between slave and free. In *The Knights,* for instance, he brings on stage all the prominent Athenian politicians of the day as slaves in the house of a bad-tempered old man called Demos: in this comedy Demosthenes' Nicias and Cleon fight, cheat, drink, spy, play the coward, curse, bawl, lie, and rant as valiantly as any slave ever born. Here the humorous aspects of servile behavior are used to make a satiric point, that the free men behave like slaves; *The Frogs* makes the opposite point by ringing the changes on the contrast between the master Dionysus and his slave Xanthias, who repeatedly exchange identities—with the surprising result that the slave emerges as his master's superior in wit, courage, and incidentally, literary taste, for Xanthias cannot abide Euripides.

In the comedy of the fourth century the magnificent fantasy and political wit of Aristophanes are sadly lacking, but the theme of contrast between slave and free remains. In the domestic comedy of Menander and his contemporaries (the models of the Roman comic poets) the theme crystallizes into a variety of stock patterns, which have exerted enormous influence on comedy ever since.

In this comedy the master design is always more or less the same. A domestic problem involving the free members of the household (usually, in Menander, a marriage or a seduction—sometimes both) is eventually solved through complicated intrigues which involve the slave members of the household. The comedy proceeds on two social levels which interpenetrate, often on two plot levels as well, which also interpenetrate. The slave characters (and a host of technically free but hardly distinguishable lower-class types such as parasites, butlers, cooks, and pimps) have their own problems (the attainment of freedom, a free meal or a free drink), the solution of which is artfully made to depend on the solution of the problem of the free characters. A typical paradigm is the plot in which a clever slave, by intelligent initiative and intrigue (often directed against his less intelligent fellow-slaves) solves his master's problem (which may range from finding a wife to marrying off a child) and, as a reward for his services, gains his private objective, his liberty.

This is a slave who has the intelligence of, and eventually attains the status of, a free man; but there is another type of slave who is a convenient vehicle for the traditional servile humor. This one provides the sullen bad temper, the cursing, the drunkenness, the indecency, thievishness, and cowardice which are the traditional characteristics of the comic slave. He may have the same ambition as his cleverer fellow, but not the same capacity; he forms grand designs, but through stupidity (often through the direct intervention of the clever slave) he fails miserably, and is humiliated and punished with blows or a stint at the mill.

While the slaves, in aspiration and action, trespass on the confines of the free world, the free-born may find themselves, as foundlings, kidnapped children, or prisoners of war, temporary denizens of the slave world; their identification and restoration to freedom (and usually marriage) is the play's denouement, and usually coincides with, and balances, the liberation of the clever slave or the restoration of the stupid slave to his proper station, or both. Together with these contrasts of condition there are deeper contrasts of nature; free men can think and act like slaves and slaves rise superior in intelligence or emotion to their masters. One of the most searching and profound of Roman comedies is Lessing's favorite, *The Captives* of Plautus, in which master and slave, both enslaved as prisoners of war, exchange identities so that the master (as the slave) can be released to take the ransom demand home, while the slave remains in slavery (as the master), risking and, as it turns out, suffering terrible punishment when the truth is discovered. The nobility displayed by the slave is, characteristically enough, justified at the end of the play by the discovery that he was really born free, and his liberation is balanced by the punishment of the slave who originally kidnapped and sold him into slavery. In this and in practically all Roman comedy, the finale is a restoration of the characters to their proper status; in the typical pattern, the restoration of one of the two young lovers to freedom makes possible their marriage, and the stern father releases the clever and independent slave who has been instrumental in bringing about the happy conclusion.

When the dramatists of the Renaissance began to imitate the Roman comedies, slavery was a thing of the past in Europe (though not a few Elizabethan worthies made their fortunes by introducing it into the West Indies), but the ancient comic design was easily adapted to the conditions of a society which, like that of Elizabethan England, was based, however insecurely, on hierarchical social categories. Shakespearian comedy abounds in brilliant adaptations of the basic formula: the cruel reduction to his proper station suffered by Malvolio, who had "greatnesse thrust" upon him; the exposure of Parolles "the gallant militarist" as a "past-saving slave"; above all the magnificent interpenetration of the two worlds of court and tavern in *Henry IV*. Falstaff acts the rôle of the King in the Boar's Head, runs his sword through Hotspur's corpse at Shrewsbury, and sets out for London crying, "The Lawes of England are at my command-ment," only to be brusquely restored to his proper station as a "Foole and Jester." Prince Hal, like some foundling, as his father suggests, begins as "sworn brother to a leash of Drawers," sounding "the very base-string of humility," but in the end re-stores himself to his proper station, "to mock the expectation of the world."

But in *The Tempest,* a Utopia which Shakespeare invented for himself (as Gonzalo invents his in the play), there is no need to translate the classic form: it can be used literally. Pros-pero is master (and incidentally an irritable old man with a marriageable daughter) and Ariel and Caliban are slaves. Pros-pero as sorcerer has the power to enslave and release the free men too: this contrast is relevant for all the characters of the play—one of its main components is what Brower has called "the slavery-freedom continuity." "The 'slaves' and 'servants' of the play," he points out, "suffer various kinds of imprisonment, from Ariel in his 'cloven pine' to Ferdinand's mild confinement, and before the end of Act IV everyone except Prospero and Mi-randa has been imprisoned in one way or another. During the course of Act V all the prisoners except Ferdinand (who has already been released) are set free. . . ." [2]

After the long expository scene between Prospero and Mi-randa (itself a typical Plautine delayed prologue) we are pre-sented with an interview between master and intelligent slave:

> All haile, great Master, grave Sir, haile: I come
> To answer Thy best pleasure; be't to fly,

[2] R. A. Brower, *The Fields of Light* (Oxford, 1951), p. 110.

> To swim, to dive into the fire: to ride
> On the curld clowds: to thy strong bidding, taske
> Ariel, and all his Qualitie.

This is servile enough, and comparable to many a hyperbolic declaration of availability made by Roman comic slaves; its comic tone is pointed up by the fact that the moment Ariel is asked to make good some of these fine promises, he rebels. "Is there more toyle?" he asks,

>   Since thou dost give me pains,
> Let me remember thee what thou hast promis'd
> Which is not yet perform'd me.
> PROSPERO: How now? moodie?
> What is't thou canst demand?
> ARIEL: My Libertie.

Some critics have been disturbed at the vehemence of Prospero's reaction; and it is true that phrases such as "Thou liest, malignant Thing"—"my slave, as thou reportst thy selfe"—and "Dull thing, I say so" sound more suited for Caliban than delicate Ariel. Yet it is not really surprising that Prospero should display what Wilson calls "ebullitions of imperious harshness" toward a slave who, after such an enthusiastic declaration of willingness to serve his, balks at the first mention of "more worke."

Prospero does more than chide; he threatens punishment. Sycorax punished Ariel with confinement in a cloven pine—"it was a torment To lay upon the damn'd"—but Prospero threatens to go one step farther: "I will rend an Oake And peg—thee in his knotty entrailes. . . ." Ariel begs for pardon and promises to be "correspondent to command." He is rewarded with a fresh promise of freedom—"after two daies I will discharge thee"— and sent about his master's business with renewed imperiousness:

> goe take this shape
> And hither come in 't: goe: hence
> With diligence.

"Exit," reads the stage direction.

From this point on Ariel is correspondent to command, and his first service is to bring Ferdinand into the presence of Miranda. It is the traditional rôle of the intelligent slave to further his master's marriage projects, and Ariel fully regains Prospero's favor and gets a renewed promise of the traditional reward. "Delicate Ariel, Ile set thee free for this." In fact, Ariel gains a remission of part of his stated time: "Ile free thee Within two dayes for this."

Throughout the rest of the play Ariel acts as Prospero's eyes and ears, but, as befits the clever slave, with a certain initiative too. He rescues Alonso and Gonzalo from the conspirators, and his words suggest that, though he has a general commission to protect Gonzalo at any rate, the methods have been left to him. "Prospero my Lord, shall know what I have done." His mischievous action against Caliban and the two Neapolitans is apparently his own idea, for Prospero later asks him where they are, and Ariel gives a full report of the chase he has led them. Yet the comic aspects of the relationship between master and slave are not neglected in the swift action of the play's central section. Ariel, ordered to produce spirits for the masque, replies:

> Before you can say come, and goe,
> And breathe twice: and cry so, so:
> Each one tripping on his Toe,
> Will be here with mop, and mowe.

This sounds remarkably like the half-ironical servile exaggeration of the Plautine slave promising miracles of speed. Charmides orders his slave to go from Athens to Piraeus—*I, i, ambula, actutum redi,* "Go on, go on, start walking, come back right away"—and gets the answer, *Illic sum atque hic sum,* "I'm there and back again." And that same Ariel who asks "Doe you love me Master? no?" at the end of the jingle quoted above, can also admit that he fears his master's temper.

> PROSPERO: Spirit: We must prepare to meet with Caliban.
> ARIEL: I my Commander, when I presented *Ceres*
> I thought to have told thee of it, but I fear'd
> Least I might anger thee.

The comic aspects of Ariel's slavery are balanced by those of Prospero's mastery. This is not the only reference to Prospero's short temper. "Why speakes my father so ungently?"—"he's compos'd of harshnesse"—"your fathers in some passion"—"never till this day Saw I him touch'd with anger, so distemper'd"—these observations only confirm the impression made by Prospero's outbursts of fury against his slaves. There is more than a touch in him of the Plautine old man, the irascible *senex* (*severus, difficilis, iratus, saevus,* as Donatus describes him),[3] who may in the end turn out to have a heart of gold, but who for the first four acts has only a noticeably short temper and a rough tongue.

This anger of Prospero is of course much more than a reminiscence of the irascibility of the stock comic figure: he is a man who has been grievously wronged, and who now, with his enemies at his mercy, intends to revenge himself. That this has been his intention is made perfectly clear in the speech in which that intention is forever renounced:

> Thogh with their high wrongs I am strook to th' quick
> Yet, with my nobler reason, gainst my furie
> Doe I take part: the rarer Action is
> In vertue, then in vengeance.

And this renunciation takes place when the slave rises superior to his master, setting an example of noble compassion:

> ARIEL: . . . your charm so strongly works 'em
> That if you now beheld them, your affections
> Would become tender.
> PROSPERO: Dost thou thinke so, Spirit?
> ARIEL: Mine would, Sir, were I humane.
> PROSPERO: And mine shall.

This is a magnificently imaginative version of the scenes in which the comedy slave surpasses the master in qualities which

[3] Cf. George F. Duckworth, *The Nature of Roman Comedy* (Princeton, 1952), p. 242, n. 14.

are traditionally those of the free man—in intelligence, courage, self-sacrifice. Here the nonhuman slave surpasses his human master in humanity.

As the play draws to a close, the recognition of Ariel's services and the renewed promises of liberation increase in frequency to become an obsessive burden:

> thou
> Shalt have the ayre at freedome: for a little
> Follow, and doe me service.
> quickly Spirit,
> Thou shalt ere long be free.
> I shall misse
> Thee, but yet thou shalt have freedome.
> Bravely (my diligence) thou shalt be free.

"The reluctance of the sylph to be under the command even of Prospero," says Coleridge, "is kept up through the whole play, and in the exercise of his admirable judgement Shakespeare has availed himself of it, in order to give Ariel an interest in the event, looking forward to that moment when he was to gain his last and only reward—simple and eternal liberty." He might have added that what Shakespeare "has availed himself of" is a dramatic design as old as European comedy.

Ariel, the slave whose nature is free, is balanced by Ferdinand, the free man and prince, who is enslaved. Accused as "spy" and "traitor," he is subdued by Prospero's magic: but there is nothing magical about the entertainment he is promised.

> Ile manacle thy necke and feete together:
> Sea water shalt thou drinke: thy food shall be

> The fresh-brooke Mussels, wither'd roots, and huskes
> Wherein the Acorne cradled. Follow.

This is a Shakespearian version of the chains and prison diet
with which the ancient comic slave is so often threatened, and
of which he so often complains. And Ferdinand's next appearance shows him performing servile tasks:

> I must remove
> Some thousands of these Logs, and pile them up,
> Upon a sore injunction.

The work he is doing is in fact Caliban's work *("Enter Caliban with a burthen of wood"* is the stage direction for the pre-
ceding scene), and Ferdinand himself describes it as "wodden
slaverie." But whereas Caliban has just declared his independence, and Ariel longs to be free, Ferdinand the free man is for
the moment content to be a slave:

> all corners else o' th' Earth
> Let liberty make use of: space enough
> Have I in such a prison.

The service which he so willingly accepts is of course not that
of his master, but that of his mistress:

> The verie instant that I saw you, did
> My heart flie to your service, there resides
> To make me slave to it, and for your sake
> Am I this patient Logge-man.

And the multiple wit of these variations on the theme is daz-
zlingly displayed when he and Miranda plight their troth:

MIRANDA: to be your fellow
You may denie me, but Ile be your servant
Whether you will or no.
FERDINAND: My Mistris (deerest)
And I thus humble ever.
MIRANDA: My husband then?
FERDINAND: I, with a heart as willing
As bondage ere of freedome: heere's my hand.

He accepts marriage (that is, bondage) with a heart "as willing as bondage ere of freedome" (as willingly as Ariel, for example, would accept his liberty), but this acceptance, overheard by Prospero, is the signal for his release from the "wodden slaverie" in which he is now bound.

Ferdinand as we have seen, is contrasted to Ariel, but Ariel's real opposite is Caliban, "my slave, who never Yeelds us kinde answere." Caliban's employment is menial: while Ariel treads "the Ooze of the salt deepe," Caliban "do's make our fire Fetch in our wood, and serves in Offices That profit us." It is remarkable that on an island where spirits can be made to produce banquets and perform masks, Prospero should need the services of Caliban to "fetch in firing . . . scrape trenchering" and "wash dish," but so it is. "We cannot misse him."

Caliban, besides being a "Tortoys," "Hag-seed," a "delicate Monster," a "Moone-calfe," a "debosh'd Fish," and a "borne Devill," is also a slave, a poisonous, lying, and abhorred slave, to quote Prospero. His first speech (offstage)—"There's wood enough within"—and the onstage curses which follow it are enough to suggest a familiar frame of reference for the first appearance of this outlandish figure: he is the surly, cursing slave of the old tradition.

Caliban's curses are highly original in expression—"language as hob-goblin as his person," says Dryden justly. Shakespeare has created a special vocabulary of invective appropriate to the savage apprehension of nature, but the expressions have the same dramatic characteristics as their venerable ancestors. The cursing seems to be a thing in and for itself—it violates plausibility, for one thing. Why should Prospero put up with it, and counter it with threats of punishment that sound curiously like it? And Caliban is made to refer to another aspect of this improbability; "his Spirits heare me, And yet I needes must curse." He "needes must curse" because his cursing is vital to the comic essence of his nature; the scene in which he exchanges curses for Prospero's threats of punishment is a traditional feature of the comedy of master and slave.

Caliban is a sullen slave (a Sceparnio), a cursing slave (a Toxilus), and he is also a lecherous one. The only touch of low sexual humor in *The Tempest* is Caliban's unrepentant laughter when reminded of his attempt on Miranda's virtue: but that one laugh is enough to remind us that he has an ancestry reaching back through scurrilous Plautine slaves and Aristophanic comic actors wearing a leather *phallos* to the ithyphallic satyrs of the Greek vase paintings.

Caliban's meeting with Trinculo and Stephano is a servile parallel and parody of Miranda's meeting with Ferdinand; both mistress and slave are overcome with wonder at the vision of their counterparts in Neapolitan society. Miranda's worshipping remark "I might call him A thing divine" is echoed in Cali-

ban's "that's a brave God, and beares Celestiall liquor"; while
Ferdinand's "My Language? Heavens" finds a base echo in
Stephano's "where the divell should he learne our language?"
Stephano and Trinculo—"two *Neapolitanes* scap'd"—are to
Ferdinand as Caliban is to Miranda; creatures of a lower order.
And Stephano the "drunken butler" is a familiar figure; the
slave in charge of his master's wine who drinks most of it himself is a standard character of the old comedy. In one of the
better-known Plautine plays, the *Miles Gloriosus,* there is a scene
with not one but two drunken butlers, one dead drunk on his
back inside the house, the other drunk on his feet outside.

But the drunkenness of Stephano is surpassed by that of Caliban. His extravagant admiration of Stephano, as Trinculo per-
ceives, is more than savage simplicity: "The poore Monster's
in drinke." In his drunken fit he thinks of the primary objective
of all slaves, his freedom. Unlike Ariel, he cannot hope to win
it by delicate service; he can gain his freedom only by working
against his master or by running away from him. He deserts
Prospero, "the Tyrant that I serve," for Stephano, and the service
of this new master turns out to be perfect freedom, which he
proceeds to celebrate in song and dance: "Freedome, high-day,
high-day, freedome." It is the traditional servile drunken exhibition and it is grotesquely funny, but it is only the other side
of the coin which shows us Ariel, moody, demanding his
liberty. Ariel and Caliban are opposite as earth and air, but
they are both enslaved, and in this they are alike. One suspects that Caliban speaks something close to the truth when
he tells Stephano that Prospero's power depends on one thing
only, his "Bookes":

> without them
> Hee's but a Sot, as I am; nor hath not
> One Spirit to command: they all do hate him
> As rootedly as I.

"They say there's but five upon this Isle," says Trinculo. "We are three of them, if th' other two be brain'd like us, the State totters." Of the three of them, the one with the most brains is Caliban. With servile flattery and cunning he supplants Trinculo in Stephano's graces, securing a series of reprimands and eventually a beating for his fellow-slave.

> Beate him enough: after a little time
> Ile beate him too.

He is now Stephano's "lieutenant," but he knows what must be done to guarantee his new-found dignity: he must encompass Prospero's death. And so the "foule Conspiracy" is formed. The slaves indulge their exaggerated fantasies of freedom and sovereignty: "Monster, I will kill this man: his daughter and I will be King and Queene, save our Graces: and *Trinculo* and Thy selfe shall be Vice-royes." It is a servile parody of the more serious conspiracy of the free men, Antonio and Sebastian.

The drunken butler dreams of a kingdom; he is not the first. It is instructive to compare his plans with those of Gripus, the Plautine slave who has fished a treasure out of the sea and intends to hang on to it:

> When I'm once free, I'll equip myself with property, an estate, a house. I'll go into trade with great ships; I'll be considered a King among Kings. . . . I'll build a great city,

and call it Gripus, after myself, a monument to my fame
and doings. And in it I'll set up a great Kingdom . . . And
yet, King though I am, I must make my breakfast on sour
wine and salt, no relish for my bread.

This comic incongruity between the present and the imagined
future, between station and ambition, is carried to hilarious
lengths in the climactic appearance of Caliban and his associates.
They "do smell all horse-pisse," but Stephano's royal dignity is
undisturbed. "Wit shall not goe unrewarded while I am King of
this Country," he says, and Trinculo hails him in the titles of the
old ballad, "O King *Stephano,* O Peere: O worthy *Stephano."*
Standing at the entrance to Prospero's cell King Stephano talks
like a tragic hero: "I do begin to have bloody thoughts." And
Caliban's urgent warnings are rejected in royal style: "Monster,
lay to your fingers . . . or Ile turne you out of my Kingdome."
  A few seconds later Stephano's kingdom melts into thin air.
And on his last appearance he and Trinculo are ordered off
with Caliban to perform menial tasks; no distinction is made
between them.

> Goe Sirha, to my Cell,
>   Take with you your Companions: as you looke
>   To have my pardon, trim it handsomely.

The stupid slaves, their wild ambitions foiled and their presump-
tion suitably punished, are restored to their proper place and
function.
  Prospero has already been recognized as "sometime *Millaine"*
and restored to *his* proper station—"thy dukedom I resigne"—

the marriage of Ferdinand and Miranda is arranged; all that remains is to free the clever slave—"to the elements Be free, and fare thou well"—and the play, except for a version of the conventional Plautine request for applause, is over, the traditional paradigm complete. Gonzalo is given the speech in which the loose ends are tied together and the pattern of restoration spelled out:

> In one voyage
> Did *Claribell* her husband finde at *Tunis,*
> And *Ferdinand* her brother, found a wife,
> Where he himselfe was lost: *Prospero* his Dukedome
> In a poore Isle:

So far we are still within the recognizable limits of the ancient plan, but Gonzalo's closing words (though they continue the metaphor of liberation) can serve to remind us that this plan is only the bare outline of a poetic structure which in feeling and imagination as far surpasses Plautine comedy as "great'st do's least":

> —*Prospero* his Dukedome
> In a poore Isle: and all of us, our selves,
> When no man was his owne.

Ray L. Heffner, Jr.

❧ UNIFYING SYMBOLS IN THE
COMEDY OF BEN JONSON

Critics since the seventeenth century have agreed that Ben Jonson is a master of comic structure, but there has been serious disagreement as to just what kind of structure it is in which he excels. To Dryden, Jonson was preeminent among English dramatists because he obeyed the neoclassic rules of unity of time, place, and action. Of the three, unity of action is fundamental, and it is Jonson's plotting that Dryden found most praiseworthy. He preferred *The Silent Woman* above all other plays because he found it an ideal combination of the scope, variety, and naturalness of the English drama with the control and careful organization of the French. And the *examen* of that play in the *Essay of Dramatic Poesy* emphasizes that there is immense variety of character and incident but that the action is "entirely one." [1] Critics in recent years, however, have disputed Dryden's picture of a regular, neoclassic Jonson, especially in the matter of plot structure. Freda L. Townsend, for example, argues persuasively that none of Jonson's great comedies has the unified action characteristic of Terentian comedy and enjoined

[1] *Essays of John Dryden,* ed. by W. P. Ker (Oxford, 1926), I, 83.

by neoclassic precept.[2] She compares Jonson's art with that of Ariosto and the baroque painters, and she sees *Bartholomew Fair* rather than *The Silent Woman* as the culmination of his development away from a simply unified comedy towards one which involves the intricate interweaving of as many different interests as possible. T. S. Eliot perhaps best sums up this "modern" view of Jonson's technique when he says that his "immense dramatic constructive skill" is not so much in plot as in "doing without a plot," and adds:

> The plot does not hold the play together; what holds the play together is a unity of inspiration that radiates into plot and personages alike.[3]

The views of Eliot and Miss Townsend seem to me substantially more correct than that of Dryden on this matter. In this paper I shall try to define more precisely the "unity of inspiration" which Eliot and others have found in Jonson's comedy and to describe the dramatic devices by which it is expressed. Briefly, I believe that the essential unity of Jonson's comedy is thematic. In each of his major plays he explores an idea or a cluster of related ideas through a variety of characters and actions. And the central expression of the unifying idea is usually not in a fully developed plot but in a fantastic comic conceit, an extravagant exaggeration of human folly, to which all of the more realistically conceived characters and incidents have reference.

[2] *Apologie for Bartholmew Fayre: the Art of Jonson's Comedies* (New York, Modern Language Association, 1947), *passim,* especially pp. 91–97.
[3] "Ben Jonson," *Elizabethan Essays* (London, 1934), p. 77.

For such an investigation the crucial cases are *The Silent Woman* and *Bartholomew Fair,* Dryden's ideal "regular" comedy and Miss Townsend's ideal "baroque" comedy. If I can show that, despite the very evident differences in superficial structure, a similar kind of thematic unity underlies each of these and that it is expressed in similar symbolic devices, my analysis may have some claim to inclusiveness.

In the case of *The Silent Woman,* I must first undertake to show that it is not, even at the level of action, held together by the "noble intrigue" as Dryden analyzes it. Dryden's spokesman Neander, accepting the definition of unity of action given earlier in the debate by Crites, tries to show that at least one English comedy adheres to the rule. Crites's principles are those derived by Renaissance and neoclassic criticism mainly from the practice of Terence. The emphasis is on the single, clearly defined aim of the action, which should be announced in the *protasis* or beginning of the play, delayed by all sorts of complications and counter-intrigues in the *epitasis* or middle, and finally brought to completion by the *catastrophe* or denouement. Neander discusses *The Silent Woman* as if it follows exactly this formula. "The action of the play is entirely one," he says, "the end or aim of which is the settling of Morose's estate on Dauphine." And he continues:

> You see, till the very last scene, new difficulties arising to obstruct the action of the play; and when the audience is brought into despair that the business can naturally be effected, then, and not before, the discovery is made.[4]

[4] Ker, *Essays of Dryden,* 1, 88.

If we consider the play in retrospect, after we have seen or read the last scene, we may agree with Neander that the securing of Morose's estate is the central aim of the whole. Dauphine's sensational revelation of the true sex of Epicoene does indeed finally and irrevocably secure for him the estate, and after the play is over we can see that all the intrigues of Truewit and Clerimont, no matter what their intended purpose, have aided Dauphine's scheme by exhausting his uncle's patience and thus making the old man desperate enough to sign the settlement. But the fact that the true nature of Dauphine's scheme is concealed until the very end makes a great difference in the kind of unity which can be perceived by the audience during the course of the play. The settling of Morose's estate on Dauphine is not the ostensible aim of the action after Act III, for the audience as well as the other characters have been led to believe that Dauphine's purposes have been fully accomplished by the marriage of Morose and Epicoene. No new difficulties arise to obstruct this action in Acts IV and V: we assume it has already been settled and our attention has turned to other matters. Even in the early acts the course of Dauphine's intrigue is remarkably smooth, and little suspense of the kind Dryden describes is generated. By the last scene, far from being brought into despair that the business of the estate can naturally be effected, we have forgotten all about it and are surprised to see it reintroduced.

As the play unfolds, the settling of Morose's estate upon Dauphine is but one among several aims which give rise to action, and it is dominant only in Act II. It is much more accurate to consider *The Silent Woman* as consisting not of a Terentian plot depending upon the delayed completion of a single, well-defined objective but of a number of separable though related actions which are initiated and brought to completion at various points in the play and which are skillfully arranged to overlap and interlock. Each of these actions is essentially a trick played on a dupe or a group of dupes, and each has four fairly well-defined stages: (1) the exposition of background material, including the characterization of the dupe; (2) the planning of the trick by the intriguer; (3) the actual execution of the trick; and (4) the reminiscence of the trick as a source of continued laughter. The general plan is that a different major action occupies the center of attention in each act except the first, which consists of exposition of material for all the actions to follow. Act II is thus centered on Dauphine's scheme to marry his uncle to Epicoene, Act III on Truewit's scheme to torment Morose by moving Sir Amorous La Foole's dinner party to Morose's house, Act IV on the double scheme to discredit the foolish knights and make all the Collegiate Ladies fall in love with Dauphine, and Act V on the tormenting of Morose through the mock discussion of marriage annulment by the pretended canon lawyer and divine.

This basic plan is complicated by the introduction of several minor actions, notably the one precipitating the disgrace of Captain Tom Otter, and by the overlapping previously mentioned. At almost every point at least three actions are under simultaneous consideration: one is at the peak of fulfillment, a second has passed its climax but is still producing laughter, and the groundwork for a third is being carefully prepared.

These sundry intrigues are connected in a number of different ways. The peculiarities of the various dupes which make them

fit objects of ridicule are all described in the course of an apparently aimless conversation in Act I, so that the jokes played
on them later in the play, though they seem to arise sponta-
neously out of particular situations, nevertheless are not unexpected. All the tricks are planned by the same group of witty
companions, most of them by Truewit, and every character has
some part in more than one intrigue. Often one intrigue depends
on the completion of another, as the transferring of the banquet
on the completion of the marriage. And the final revelation of
Epicoene's sex, as Miss Townsend points out, has some relevance to all the major actions; [5] it not only accomplishes Morose's
divorce and gains the estate for Dauphine, it also shows the
foolish knights to be liars and discomfits the Collegiate Ladies,
who have had to depend on a despised male for the vindication
of their honors.

Such an elaborate intertwining of episodes demonstrates great
technical skill in what Renaissance criticism called *disposition*
and *economy*.[6] But we are still entitled to ask, is this the only
kind of structure the play possesses? Are there no more fundamental relationships among these various characters and actions,
of which the mechanical interconnections we have been discussing are but the external evidences? The thematic structure of
the play will be clearer if we consider that its real center is not
in any of the tricks or schemes but in the ridiculous situation

[5] Townsend, *Bartholmew Fayre,* p. 64.

[6] In his *Discoveries* (lines 1815–20 in the Herford and Simpson edition) Jonson
speaks slightingly of Terence's skill in these matters, though it was much praised
by most Renaissance critics. For the meaning of the terms, see Marvin T. Herrick,
Comic Theory in the Sixteenth Century ("Illinois Studies in Language and Literature," Vol. XXXIV, Nos. 1–2 [Urbana, 1950]), pp. 94–106.

in which Morose finds himself. My argument is not genetic, but a brief look at the probable sources of the play may help to confirm this impression. The sources of the separable parts are extremely varied. Passages of dialogue come from Juvenal and Ovid, many of the characters belong in the series of satiric portraits stretching back through Jonson's early plays and through contemporary nondramatic satire; the aborted duel between the two knights seems to come from *Twelfth Night,* the conflict between Dauphine and his uncle bears some resemblance to *A Trick to Catch the Old One,* and the device of trickery through concealed sex may come from Aretino's comedy *Il Marescalco.*[7] But the center around which all this material is arranged is clearly the comic conceit which Jonson took from a declamation of Libanius—the ludicrous plight of a noise-hating man married by fraud to a noisy woman.

Herford and Simpson observe that, "The amusing oration of Libanius offered but slender stuff for drama."[8] This is true enough, in that it contained only a situation and not a complete plot, and the implications of that situation were but little developed. The Morosus of Libanius merely describes the horrors of his noise-ridden existence and pleads with the judges for permission to commit suicide. The oration could not simply be translated to the stage without the addition of much extra material. But it is, nevertheless, an admirable idea for a comedy.

---

[7] For these and other sources see C. H. Herford and Others, *Ben Jonson* (Oxford, 1925–52), II, 72–79 (1925), and the notes in Vol. x (1950); also the edition by Julia Ward Henry ("Yale Studies in English," No. xxxi [New York, 1906]), pp. xxviii–lvi, and O. J. Campbell, "The Relation of *Epicoene* to Aretino's *Il Marescalco,*" *PMLA,* xlvi (1931), 752–62.

[8] *Ben Jonson,* II, 76 (1925).

For one thing, it epitomizes the eternal battle of the sexes for supremacy, including the hypocrisies of courtship and the wrangling after marriage. And then also, in its opposition of noisy people to noise haters, it suggests another eternal theme, the debate between the active and the quiet life. In constructing a play around the conceit of Libanius, Jonson greatly complicates both these latent themes, through his interpretation of the Morose-Epicoene relationship and through the addition of other characters and actions.

Jonson's interpretation of the central situation is summarized in the scene in which Morose interrogates his intended bride. (ii.v.) There we learn that the old man's hatred of noise is the outward manifestation of two allied character traits. First, he has been at court and has recoiled in horror from all forms of courtliness. He tests his bride-to-be by pointing out to her that if she forbear the use of her tongue she will be unable to trade "pretty girds, scoffes, and daliance" with her admirers; she cannot, like the ladies in court, "affect . . . to seeme learn'd, to seeme judicious, to seeme sharpe, and conceited"; and she will be manifestly unable to "have her counsell of taylors, lineners, lacewomen, embroyderers, and sit with 'hem sometimes twise a day, upon *French* intelligences" so as "to be the first and principall in all fashions." The meaning of the play's central symbol of noise is thus considerably developed in this scene; a noisy woman is a woman given over to all the vanity, hypocrisy, and affectation to which her sex and the courtly society of her age are prone. Morose can concentrate his hatred of all these things by hating the inclusive and concrete symbol, noise itself.

The second important aspect of Morose's idiosyncracy is his

passion for having his own way in all things. In his first soliloquy
he admits that "all discourses, but mine owne, afflict mee." (II.
i.) He admires the absolute obedience which oriental potentates
command from members of their households; and the silence of
his own servants indicates their complete subservience to his will,
for they can answer perfectly well by signs so long as their judgments "jump" with his. Epicoene thus throws him into ecstasies
of happiness when she answers to all his questions, "Judge you,
forsooth," and "I leave it to wisdome, and you sir."

Morose's attitude towards his nephew illustrates both these
aspects of his character. After putting his intended bride success-
fully through the test, he breaks into a scornful tirade at the
notion of Sir Dauphine's knighthood:

> He would be knighted, forsooth, and thought by that meanes
> to raigne over me, his title must doe it: no kinsman, I will
> now make you bring mee the tenth lords, and the sixteenth
> ladies letter, kinsman; and it shall doe you no good kins-
> man. Your knighthood it selfe shall come on it's knees, and
> it shall be rejected. (II.v.)

By the coup of his marriage, Morose hopes to express his contempt for all the world of lords, ladies, and courtly society, as
well as his complete dominance over all members of his family.
The comic irony in his situation is that he inevitably brings all
his troubles on himself, because his two desires, to command and
to live apart, though so closely related, cannot both be fulfilled
on his terms. An ascetic hermit might live apart and rail against
the court; a great lord might command absolute obedience from
all around him. But Morose will make no sacrifice; he will be

the ultimate of both at once. In seeking to extend his circle of
dominance beyond his servant and his barber to include a
wife, he brings in upon himself the torrent of courtly commotion from which he has fled. In seeking to make his power
over his nephew absolute, he loses all. When Dauphine says to
him at the end of the play, "Now you may goe in and rest, be
as private as you will, sir," his sarcastic words may seem more
than a little cruel, but it is the logic of the world that decrees
Morose's sentence. He can be "private" only when he gives up
all pretense of being an absolute autocrat, and this he has just
done by submitting himself humbly to his nephew's will and
judgment.

The other material in the play consists largely of a set of mirrors which, by reflecting various aspects of this central situation, extend its significance. The Collegiate Ladies, for example, are embodiments of all the courtly vices and affectations
which Morose lumps under the heading of "female noise." The
most prominent feature of their composite portrait is, in
Morose's words, that they "affect to seem judicious." As Truewit
says in the first act,

> [They are] an order betweene courtiers, and country-madames,
> that live from their husbands; and give entertainement to
> all the *Wits,* and *Braveries* o' the time, as they call 'hem:
> crie downe, or up, what they like, or dislike in a braine, or
> a fashion, with most masculine, or rather *hermaphroditicall*
> authoritie. (I.i.)

The Collegiates are thus an appropriate part of the flood of
noise that pours in upon Morose after the wedding through

which he had hoped to assert his masculine dominance and to declare his independence from all courtliness. The ladies' pretense to authority is just as absurd as Morose's. This is demonstrated in Act IV by the disgrace of the two knights whom they had cried up as wits and braveries, and especially by the ease with which the ladies can be turned from one opinion to its exact opposite, from idolizing the two knights to despising them, from despising Dauphine to being infatuated with him. As Truewit says, his tricks prove that

> all their actions are governed by crude opinion, without reason or cause; they know not why they doe any thing: but as they are inform'd, beleeve, judge, praise, condemne, love, hate, and in aemulation one of another, doe all these things alike. (IV.vi.)

Sir John Daw and Sir Amorous La Foole are the male representatives of the affected courtliness which Morose despises. In contrast to the three ladies, these two have separate identities at the beginning, though they are merged into a composite portrait as the action progresses. Sir John is the "wit" or fool intellectual, Sir Amorous the "bravery" or fool social. Jonson had treated varieties of both in earlier plays, but he fits these into his present scheme by emphasizing in both cases the noisiness of their folly. Sir John is the "onely talking sir i'th' towne" whom Truewit dares not visit for the danger to his ears. His conversation is noise not only because it is verbose but also because it is inopportune and disorderly. He insists upon reading his wretched verses, whether or not the company desires to hear them; he pours out the names of authors in an undisciplined stream. The garrulity of Sir Amorous has similar characteristics though different subject matter. Clerimont emphasizes that this knight's pretentious courtesy respects neither place, person, nor season:

> He will salute a Judge upon the bench, and a Bishop in the pulpit, a Lawyer when hee is pleading at the barre, and a Lady when shee is dauncing in a masque, and put her out. He do's give playes, and suppers, and invites his guests to 'hem, aloud, out of his windore, as they ride by in coaches. (i.iii.)

When Sir Amorous appears on the scene, he does, as Clerimont has predicted, "tell us his pedigree, now; and what meat he has to dinner; and, who are his guests; and, the whole course of his fortunes," all in one breath.

The two knights thus give a wider meaning to the notion of a noisy man in much the same way as the Collegiates and Morose's interrogation of Epicoene widen the meaning of a noisy woman. Noise is ungentlemanly boasting about one's poetic and critical powers, about one's family, friends, and hospitality, and, towards the end of the play, about one's sexual powers and conquests. The one gentlemanly attribute to which the two do not conspicuously pretend is courage on the field of battle. We may therefore be somewhat puzzled when the main trick against them seems to turn on their cowardice, and we sympathize with Mrs. Doll Mavis when she defends her judgment of them by saying, "I commended but their wits, madame, and their braveries. I never look'd toward their valours." (iv.vi.) But what has been exposed in the mock duel is not only cowardice but pliability. Like the ladies who admire them, the knights have no real standards for judging either books or men, but are governed entirely by rumor and fashion. Therefore it is ridiculously easy for Truewit to persuade each knight that the other, whose pacific disposition he should know well, is a raging lion thirsting for his blood. If either knight had been made more on the model of the swaggering *miles gloriosus,* the point about how easy it is to make a fool believe the exact opposite of the obvious truth would have been blunted.

The themes of courtly behavior, the battle between the sexes, and the pretense to authority are intertwined with that of noise versus silence wherever one looks in the play, even in the foolish madrigals of modesty and silence written by Sir John Daw. In the action involving Captain and Mrs. Tom Otter, all these subjects are invested with an atmosphere of comedy lower than that of the rest of the play. For the salient fact about the Otters is that they are of a lower social class than any of the other main characters. Mrs. Otter is a rich China woman struggling for admission to the exclusive Ladies' College; Captain Tom is at home among the bulls and bears but unsure of himself in the company of knights and wits. Here again the citizen-couple who welcome instruction in the courtly follies are familiar figures from Jonson's early comical satire, but the portraits are modified to fit the thematic pattern of this play. The Collegiate Ladies may pretend to a nice discernment in brains and fashions, but Mrs. Otter comprehends fashionable feminism rather differently and expresses her "masculine, or rather *hermaphroditicall* authority" more elementally by pummeling her husband. And Captain Tom's noises are his boisterous but rather pathetic drinking bouts, accompanied by drum and trumpet, by which he hopes to gain a reputation among the gentry and to assert his independence from his wife. This is the comic realm of Maggie and Jiggs, the hen-pecked husband sneaking out to the corner saloon to escape his social-climbing wife, but the relationships between this farcical situation and the central one of Morose and Epicoene are clear and are emphasized at every turn. Like the characters in most Elizabethan comic sub-plots, the Otters burlesque the main action while at the same time extending its meaning toward the universal.

As the clumsy, middle-class Otters contrast with the more assured aristocrats, so all the pliable pretenders to courtliness contrast with the true gentlemen and scholars, Truewit, Clerimont, and Dauphine. Within this group of intriguers, however, there is a further important contrast. Clerimont is relatively undeveloped as a character, but the differences between Truewit and Dauphine are stressed. Truewit is boisterous and boastful about the jokes he contrives. He must have the widest possible audience; as Dauphine tells him, "This is thy extreme vanitie, now: thou think'st thou wert undone, if every jest thou mak'st were not publish'd." (iv.v.) Dauphine, on the other hand, moves quietly about his purposes and keeps his own counsel. Truewit characteristically invents his fun on the spur of the moment, out of the materials at hand, and is apt to promise to do something (like making all the Collegiates fall in love with Dauphine) before he has the slightest idea how it can be brought about. Dauphine's plans have been months in preparation, and he betrays little hint of his purposes until they actually have been accomplished.

The rivalry of these two for the title of master plotter runs as a subdued motive through all the action. It is most prominent in the first two acts, when Truewit's rash and suddenly conceived scheme to dissuade Morose from marrying almost upsets Dauphine's carefully laid plot. It might seem that the contrast is all in favor of the quiet, modest, but in the end more effective Dauphine. Truewit assumes too readily that he can read the entire situation at first glance, and that he can easily manipulate the stubborn Morose. He becomes almost a comic butt himself when he ridiculously tries to pretend that he has foreseen from the first the really quite unexpected consequence of his action. The denouement especially would seem to prove that Dauphine is the real master at playing chess with characters and humors, and Truewit just the bungling amateur. But Jonson is not writing a treatise after the manner of Plutarch on the virtue of silence and the folly of garrulity. Dauphine and Truewit share the honors in the closing scene, and there is more than a little to be said throughout the play for Truewit's engaging love of good fun for its own sake as against Dauphine's colder, more practical scheming. Instead of arguing a simple thesis, Jonson is investigating another aspect of his central symbol of noise. Just as he holds a brief neither for the noise of courtly affectation nor for Morose's extreme hatred of it, so he argues neither for the noisy wit nor for the quiet wit but is content to explore the differences between them.

The essential movement of *The Silent Woman,* then, is the exploration of themes implicit in the central comic conceit of a noise-hating man married to a noisy woman. Noise and the hatred of noise take on the proportion of symbols as they are given ever-widening meanings by the various particulars of social satire. The play's realism and its fantastic caricature can hardly be disentangled, for they are held together firmly in the same comic structure.

Much the same things can be said of *Bartholomew Fair,* despite its even greater complexity and its different kind of surface plan. In this play, characters, actions, interests are all multiplied. If in *The Silent Woman* there are usually three separable intrigues in motion at the same time, they all have a similar pattern of development and are under the control of no more than three intriguers. But in *Bartholomew Fair* five or six actions seem always to be ripening simultaneously, there are more than a dozen intriguers, and no single pattern of development will fit all the kinds of action which the fair breeds. Jonson, however, adheres to a firm if complicated plan in devising the apparent chaos of his fair, and this play has a thematic structure much like that of *The Silent Woman.* Here again Jonson is not arguing a thesis but is investigating diverse aspects of a central problem; here again the various parts of his play are used to mirror each other; and here again the "unity of inspiration" is best expressed by a character who is a fantastic caricature, in an extremely absurd situation which is reflected by all the more "realistic" figures in the play.

The central theme is the problem of what "warrant" men have or pretend to have for their actions. The problem touches both epistemology and ethics—the questions of how we know what we think we know, and why we behave as we do. Stated thus, it is very broad indeed, but it is brought into focus by several concrete symbols of legal sanction. The Induction, for example, is built on the device of a formal contract between the playwright and the audience, giving the customers license to judge the play, but only within specified limits. The play itself opens with Proctor John Littlewit discussing a marriage license taken out by Bartholomew Cokes and Grace Wellborn, and the possession of this document becomes of central importance not only in gulling the testy "governor" Humphrey Wasp but also in the "romantic" plot involving Grace, the two witty gallants, and Dame Purecraft.

The most important symbol of this basic theme, however, is the "warrant" which the madman Troubleall demands of almost all the characters in the fourth act. This demented former officer of the Court of Pie-Powders, who has neither appeared nor been mentioned earlier in the play, is obsessed with the necessity of documentary sanction for even the slightest action. As the watchman Bristle explains, Troubleall will do nothing unless he has first obtained a scrap of paper with Justice Overdo's name signed to it:

> He will not eate a crust, nor drinke a little, nor make him in his apparell, ready. His wife, Sirreverence, cannot get him make his water, or shift his shirt, without his warrant. (iv.i.)

In Troubleall's absurd humor we have the same kind of grand, extravagant comic conceit as that provided by Morose's hatred of all noise. It is the ultimate extreme, the fantastic caricature of the widespread and not unnatural human craving for clearly defined authority, and it serves as the most significant unifying device in the play. Troubleall intervenes crucially in several of the threads of plot, settling the dispute between Grace's lovers, freeing Overdo and Busy from the stocks, and enabling Quarlous to cheat Justice Overdo and marry the rich widow Purecraft. But beyond his service as a catalyst of action, Trouble-all's main function is, as his name suggests, to trouble everybody as he darts suddenly on and off the stage with his embarrassing question, "Have you a warrant for what you do?" This leads to a reexamination of the motives of all the characters, a new scrutiny of what warrant they really have and what they pretend to have for their beliefs and their deeds.

Neither the outright fools nor the outright knaves are much troubled by the great question. The booby Cokes, who has never sought a reason for anything he did, exclaims scornfully, "As if a man need a warrant to lose any thing with!" And Wasp, who pretends to "judgment and knowledge of matters" but who really is just as much motivated by irrational whim as his foolish pupil, cries out during the game of vapours, "I have no reason, nor I will heare of no reason, nor I will looke for no reason, and he is an Asse, that either knowes any, or lookes for't from me." (IV.iv.) Among the knaves, Edgeworth the cutpurse is jolted for a moment by Troubleall's question, thinking that his villainy has been found out, but he quickly returns to planning his next robbery. Most resolute of all is the pimp Knockem, who immediately sits down and *forges* Trouble-all a warrant for whatever he may want. As Cokes is motivated by sheer whim, so the sharpers of the fair are motivated by sheer desire for gain, and neither feels the need for further justification.

The watchmen Haggis and Bristle, however, who are on the

fringes of the fair's knavery, are led to reflect that Justice
Overdo is "a very parantory person" who can get very angry
indeed when he has a mind to, "and when hee is angry, be it
right or wrong; hee has the Law on's side, ever." (IV.i.) In
other words, "warrant" for the watchmen is contained entirely
in the unpredictable personality of the judge whom they serve;
they have no concern with the guilt or innocence of those whom
they incarcerate, and if there is ethics behind the law, they do
not comprehend it.

Justice Overdo himself has a double function in the play. For
the watchmen and for Troubleall, his name stands as a symbol
for the ultimate authority which requires no rational understanding. But as a character in the action, Overdo has his own
"warrants" for his conduct, and they are neither irrational nor
hypocritical. His motives—to protect the innocent and reprehend
the guilty—are beyond reproach; nor is his reliance for his general ethics upon Stoic philosophy as expounded by the Roman
poets in itself anything but admirable. And he has the further
laudable desire to base his judicial decisions on exact information; he will trust no spies, foolish constables, or sleepy watchmen, but will visit the fair in disguise, to search out enormities
for himself at first hand. But for all this the Justice is completely
ineffectual, because he cannot interpret correctly what he sees,
and because he fails to differentiate between the minor vani-
ties and major iniquities of the fair. Many are the yearly enormities of the place, as he says, but he concentrates on the evils
of bottle-ale, tobacco, and puppet shows and fails to see the
robbery and seduction going on under his nose. Even when he
taxes the right knaves, it is for the wrong crimes. Through the

characterization of Justice Overdo, Jonson seems to me to add the warning that even the best of warrants is not in itself sufficient to insure right action; Overdo is reminded at the end that his first name is Adam and he is but flesh and blood, subject to error like the rest of us. Even such admirable principles as reverence for the classics and reliance upon the facts of evidence can, if adhered to blindly, become fetishes almost as ludicrous as Troubleall's trust in a signature.

The application of the theme of warrant to Rabbi Zeal-of-the-Land Busy, who pretends to find authority for everything he does in the words of scripture but who really is motivated by the most elemental greed and gluttony, and whose ingenious discovery of theological reasons for the consumption of roast pig by the faithful is perhaps the funniest scene in the entire play, need not be further elaborated. The most interesting *effects* of Troubleall's persistent questioning are those upon Dame Purecraft and upon Quarlous. The Puritan widow is seized with a frenzied desire to reform; the witty gentleman comes close to becoming an outright knave.

For Dame Purecraft, Troubleall's madness seems the only possible alternative to the life of double dealing she has been leading. She exclaims:

> Mad doe they call him! the world is mad in error, but hee is mad in truth. . . . O, that I might be his yoake-fellow, and be mad with him, what a many should wee draw to madnesse in truth, with us! (iv.vi.)

"Madness in error" in the specific case of Dame Purecraft means reliance upon the Puritan interpretation of Biblical authority. In the first scene of Act IV she had replied confidently to Trouble-all's question, "Yes, I have a warrant out of the word." But now she admits freely that her adherence to scriptural authority was but subterfuge for wicked self-seeking, and she wants to exchange her hypocritical Puritanism for the absolute and ingenuous madness which Troubleall represents. The final irony is that she gains for a husband not a real madman but a gentleman-rogue disguised as a lunatic, Quarlous tricked out for his own selfish purposes in the clothes of Troubleall. Even the search for pure irrationality thus turns out to be futile; Dame Purecraft is yoked with the image of her former self, and her glorious repentance and conversion have been in vain.

Quarlous comes to a similar conclusion that the only choice is between knavery and madness, but he has little hesitation in choosing knavery. As he stands aside to deliberate Dame Purecraft's proposal, he reasons thus:

> It is money that I want, why should I not marry the money, when 'tis offer'd mee? I have a *License* and all, it is but razing out one name, and putting in another. There's no playing with a man's fortune! I am resolv'd! I were truly mad, an' I would not! (v.ii.)

And so he proceeds not only to marry the rich widow but also to extract money by fraud from Justice Overdo, from his erstwhile friend Winwife, and from Grace, the girl for whom he has so recently declared his love. The warrant which Quarlous abandons is the code of a gentleman, including the chivalric ideals of loyalty to one's friend and undying devotion to one's mistress. But the movement of the play here as elsewhere is towards the discovery of true motives rather than towards change of character, for though Quarlous has loudly protested both love and friendship, he has never really been governed by either.

Quarlous' mode of thinking and of acting approaches more and more closely that of those absolute rogues, the inhabitants of the fair. And Quarlous is just as loud in protesting his difference from the fair people as Humphrey Wasp is in protesting his difference from his foolish pupil. Quarlous resents being greeted familiarly by such rascals as Knockem and Whit, and in a very revealing passage he first lashes out at the cutpurse Edgeworth for treating him like one of "your companions in beastlinesse." He then proceeds to find excuses for having been accessory before and after the fact to a robbery:

> Goe your wayes, talke not to me, the hangman is onely fit to discourse with you. . . . I am sorry I employ'd this fellow; for he thinks me such: *Facinus quos inquinat, aequst.* But, it was for sport. And would I make it serious, the getting of this Licence is nothing to me, without other circumstances concurre. (IV.vi.)

This is a piece of rationalization worthy of the master, Rabbi Busy; and we observe with some amusement that Quarlous immediately starts taking steps to *make* the other circumstances concur through fraud.

The emphasis in *Bartholomew Fair* is thus on the narrow range of motives that actually govern men's actions, in contrast to the wide variety of warrants which they pretend to have. Notable prominence is given to primitive motivations: Busy scents after pork like a hound, both Mrs. Littlewit and Mrs.

Overdo are drawn into the clutches of the pimps by the necessity for relieving themselves, and the longing of a pregnant woman is the ostensible reason which sets the whole Littlewit party in motion towards the fair. As the many hypocrisies are revealed, the only distinction which seems to hold up is that between fools and knaves, between Cokes and the rogues who prey on him. The other characters are seen as approaching more and more closely to these extremes, until all search for warrant seems as absurd as Troubleall's, since all authority is either as corrupt as the watchmen or as irrational as Wasp or as blind as Justice Overdo. Whim, animal appetite, and sordid greed have complete sway over men's actions without as well as within the fair; the fair merely provides the heightened conditions under which disguises fall off and the elemental motivations become manifest.

In both the plays we have been considering then, fantastic exaggerations like Morose's hatred of noise and Troubleall's search for a warrant provide the lenses through which the behavior of more realistically conceived characters can be observed and brought into focus. It is chiefly in his grand comic conceits that Jonson's "unity of inspiration" resides, for in them the interplay of realistic satire and fantastic caricature is most highly concentrated, and from them it does truly "radiate into plot and personages alike."

It is this interplay between realism and fantasy which seems to me the very essence of Jonson's comedy. To decry, as Herford and Simpson do, the prominence of the "farcical horror-of-noise-motive" in *The Silent Woman,* and to regret the "deep-seated contrarieties in Jonson's own artistic nature, where the bent of a great realist for truth and nature never overcame the satirist's and humorist's weakness for fantastic caricature" [9] is, I believe, seriously to misunderstand Jonson's art. His purpose was always to hold the mirror up to nature, but not simply to present the world of common experience, uncriticized and unstructured. Without the extravagant caricatures which he develops into organizing symbols, Jonson's comedy would lack not only the unity but also the universality of great art.

If Jonson's comedy is of the sort here suggested, then a comparison with Aristophanes may not be amiss. Here again we have a mingling of fantasy and realism, and here again we have a comic structure centered not on a plot but on the exploration of an extravagant conceit. Jonson has almost always been discussed as if he belonged in the tradition of Menander, Plautus, and Terence—of New Comedy. I believe that we might gain more insight into his art if we considered him instead in the quite different tradition of Old Comedy. Perhaps Jonson meant more than we have given him credit for meaning when he said of the comedy he was working to develop that it was not bound by Terentian rules but was "of a particular kind by itself, somewhat like *Vetus Comoedia.*" [10]

[9] *Ben Jonson,* II, 76–78 (1925).
[10] Induction to *Every Man out of His Humour.*

◄§ RESTORATION COMEDY AND LATER

The high reputation of Restoration comedy has been sustained on surprisingly slight critical authority. It is true that the squeamishness of the two centuries following *The Way of the World* prevented more than an occasional outraged dismissal, or defensive impressionistic survey, of what was taken (except, disingenuously, by Lamb) for the accurate reflection of a debauched society. Critics during the past several decades have had no such excuse. The inhibition removed, we expect due and favorable examination of the age of Wycherley and Congreve. The most persuasive recent examination, however, is an attack, by L. C. Knights; and Mr. Knights is not squeamish, but bored: "The criticism . . . [their] defenders . . . need to answer is not that the comedies are 'immoral,' but that they are trivial, gross and dull." [1]

It may be said for the defenders that they, at least, are not bored with this "finely polished art of the intellect that gives us amply in return for the vulgarity." [2] They find the novel virtue of the Restoration comic dramatist in his "desire to try new ways

[1] *Explorations* (New York, 1947), "Restoration Comedy: The Reality and the Myth," p. 168.

[2] A. Nicoll, *Restoration Drama* (4th ed., Cambridge, 1952), p. 201.

of living"; [3] they explore his preoccupation with "life . . . accepted and observed—not as a problem, but a pageant"; [4] they single out his invention of "personalities" of "unfailing grace and distinction," to which the "thoroughly conventionalized social mode" of the court of Charles II "could not give complete expression"; [5] they confide that in the contemplation of his plays "we become for the moment pagan, without a thought of the morrow, existing solely for the joy of the hour." [6] They can also penetrate, through a modish generalization by Congreve's Angelica on the pleasures of the sex-chase ("Uncertainty and expectation are the joys of life," etc.), to the heart and *Weltschmerz* of Restoration comedy:

> This is not the observation of a jilt, of a baggage without sensibility, but of a woman who has known and suffered, who has been disappointed in her early estimate of things. It is the weary cry of the knower who realizes that happiness may not be sought for or grasped, and that joy must be snatched as it flies. These were not mere puppets, but breathing, living, desiring men and women. [7]

From such throbbing appreciation it is salutary to turn back to the plays themselves and to agree with Mr. Knights. Certainly Restoration comedy lacks the "quality and variety," the vigor and scope, of interest and idiom that the Elizabethan

[3] B. Dobrée, *Restoration Comedy* (Oxford, 1926), p. 22.

[4] J. Palmer, *The Comedy of Manners* (London, 1913), p. 191.

[5] K. M. Lynch, *The Social Mode of Restoration Comedy* (New York, 1926), pp. 181, 216.

[6] Nicoll, *Restoration Drama*, p. 200.

[7] Dobrée, *Restoration Comedy*, p. 137.

playwrights, for example, could draw upon. In Restoration wit "the verbal pattern appears at times to be completely unrelated to a mode of perceiving," the words "have an air of preening themselves on their acute discriminations," though "the antitheses are mechanical, and the pattern is monotonously repeated." "In the matter of sexual relations Restoration comedy is entirely dominated by a narrow set of conventions," and even these conventions the dramatist does not, characteristically, examine in order to trace and predict the directions they may give to human impulses. Rather, he exploits them in order to gratify "the constant need for titillation" of an inanely artificial society "lacking the real sophistication and self-knowledge that might, in some measure, have redeemed it." [8]

Still, the indictment may not be so damaging as it seems. Mr. Knights's least disputable charge, concerning the inferiority of Restoration to Elizabethan drama, reminds us that, whatever their relative merits, each of them was authoritative enough to define its age as an age of drama—the rarest kind of literary age—during which a number of playwrights, united by a community of conventions and interests and identifiable by common qualities of idiom and style, not only hold the stage but dominate the writing of their time. Aside from the century of Shakespeare and Congreve, there is indeed no English literary period with a surviving, not to mention dominating, drama. Mr. Knights's comparison may imply, then, more odium than it should: the fact that the Restoration theater is, by the standard of the Elizabethan, unresourceful and limited must be seen in the light of the equally unarguable fact that, though the

[8] Knights, *Explorations, passim.*

English stage has had other names and other entertainments, it has had no other theater at all.

As for the superiority of Elizabethan *comedy* to Wycherley and Congreve, that is altogether arguable. "The fault . . . of Shakespeare's comic Muse," remarked Hazlitt, "is . . . that it is too good-natured and magnanimous." It is scarcely unorthodox to suggest that Shakespeare's comic figures are for the most part either casually witty observers or the merest butts, and that his "comedies" are good-natured mélanges always ready to sacrifice any dramatic pattern—including the comic patterns of mechanism and vitality, plausibility and substance, deceit and exposure—in order to examine the margin of humanness, the strong (and at times dramatically fatal) pathos discoverable by Shakespeare in Malvolio and Shylock as well as in Shallow and Falstaff. The so-called "problem comedies"—*Measure for Measure* and *Troilus and Cressida,* especially—are in fact Shakespeare's solution of his comic problem: they are irreducible tragicomedies, in which Shakespeare creates a form hospitable to the pathos and self-exhausting complexity of motive that he constantly discovers in protagonists not quite grand or lucky enough to be tragic.

The claim of Elizabethan comedy must rest, eventually, with Jonson, who lacked Shakespeare's talent for pathos and Fletcher's weakness for it and was therefore unimpelled to make new genres or to corrupt old ones. The contribution of Jonson's audience was the Elizabethan delight in roguery—we have the testimony of the pamphleteers and "true-history" writers as well as the dramatists—and nothing is more susceptible to the logic of comedy than the cycle of deception and self-deception, exposure and mortification between rogue and gull or between rogue and rogue, the innocent dishonest dream of something for nothing, the most enduring symbol of which is Jonson's own Alchemist. What Jonson himself contributed was the virtue of his defect: incapable of pathos, he is supremely capable of reducing motive to monomania and so diverting attention from the players to the gusto and intricate strategy of the game itself—the game, that is, of comedy, in which there are the manipulated and the manipulators, dupedom and the triumphant or foiled ingenuity of conscious appetite.

Jonson's power is dramatic; it affirms itself primarily, not in scene-shifting or stage-business, but in language. Even the live precision and tension of his plot grow out of the sardonic precision of his verse, as if everything—in *this* comic world at least —can be said directly, as if every purpose proclaims itself. It is a language of perfect transparency in which self-recognition is offered to all, as when Mosca flatters the lawyer, one of Volpone's would-be heirs:

> I oft have heard him say how he admir'd
> Men of your large profession, that could speak
> To every cause, and things mere contraries,
> Till they were hoarse again, yet all be law;
> That, with most quick agility, could turn
> And return; make knots, and undo them;
> Give forked counsel; take provoking gold
> On either hand, and put it up; these men,
> He knew, would thrive with their humility.
> And, for his part, he thought he should be blest

> To have his heir of such a suffering spirit,
> So wise, so grave, of so perplex'd a tongue,
> And loud withal, that would not wag, nor scarce
> Lie still, without a fee. . . .

It is a language in which man can even take the measure of his own desires, as when Sir Epicure, awaiting from the Alchemist the promised philosopher's stone, prophesies his own creatable paradise:

> I will have all my beds blown up, not stuff'd:
> Down is too hard; and then, mine oval room
> Fill'd with such pictures as Tiberius took
> From Elephantis, and dull Aretine
> But coldly imitated. Then, my glasses
> Cut in more subtle angles, to disperse
> And multiply the figures, as I walk
> Naked between my succubae. My mists
> I'll have of perfume, vapour'd 'bout the room,
> To lose our selves in; and my baths, like pits
> To fall into; from whence we will come forth,
> And roll us dry in gossamer and roses. . . .

It is a language, like Chaucer's or Swift's, rooted in an idiom rich with particular moral values—the ground of agreement between author and audience—and freely expressive of any moral deviations that human impulse contrives. It may be, indeed, the very freedom and particularity of the idiom that tempt Jonson—even in *Volpone* and *The Alchemist*—to scatter his shots with conversational exuberance, to indulge at times a strenuous self-righteousness (as through the straw figures of purity that he sets up against his energetic Vices), to stray out of comedy into topical satire, to aim at easy irrelevant targets like Sir Politic Would-Be. The Elizabethan tendency to this sort of logorrhea (so feelingly pointed out in Shakespeare by Jonson himself) is a tendency that makes even the best of Jonson's comedies blur at the edges. Wycherley—in *The Country Wife* at least—attending to similar comic deceits and disclosures, taking off from a device very similar to the initiatory device in *Volpone,* and working for the most part with characters obviously conceived as Jonsonian humours, manages to achieve a tough precision comparable to Jonson's; the achievement is on a smaller scale doubtless, but without Jonson's waste and misfire; and the conventions, however narrow, of the Restoration theater and the Restoration audience may be in part responsible.

In *Volpone* and *The Alchemist,* the two principal themes are avarice and lust, which are for Jonson—and his audience—moral deviations not only grave but almost inseparable, as though one inevitably implies the other; and if this mingling of sins seems to draw on the strength of the Christian-ethical tradition (which after all concerns itself with men and not comic figures), it also divides the attention and weakens Jonson's central comic effect: the clutter of single obsessions maneuvering and colliding. Like many other Elizabethan dramatists, Jonson suffers from a surplus of themes, a superabundance of interests that he shares with his audience.

By the time of the Restoration, however, the popular audience of Jonson (and Shakespeare), already dwindling with the spread of Puritan sympathies during the Caroline period, had vanished entirely. Wycherley's spectators were "the courtiers and their satellites," [9] and for such an idle and fashionable group, certain of Jonson's themes would have appeared barbarous and dull. For the Restoration audience, lust was, fashionably, little more than a casuistical Puritan distinction; and avarice was a tiresome trait hardly worth discussing among gentlemen or representing on a civilized stage—a trait of shopkeepers. (The latter, regarding the theaters as no better than brothels, never paid the price of admission and so did not have to be appeased.) For such an audience—without occupation, consciously straining toward an ideal of heroically casual debauchery, setting out to make up for the lost years under the Commonwealth—perhaps the only possible theme and motive was sex, that neutral stuff which the Elizabethans had graded into love and lust but which might now subside into unity again.

A dramatist is far more likely, in any case, to be numbed than invigorated by the prescriptions of theme and motive that his audience imposes and anticipates. Certainly, just as Elizabethan tragedy is in its mass a hodgepodge of butchery and tattered passions, so Restoration comedy is, in its overwhelming mass, a hodgepodge of premature sophistications, of inert, self-admiring wit and resolutely impertinent reversals of established sexual

[9] "The noblemen in the pit and boxes, the fops and beaux and wits or would-be-wits who hung on to their society, the women of the court, depraved and licentious as the men, the courtesans with whom these women of quality moved and conversed as on equal terms, made up at least four-fifths of the entire audience. Add a sprinkling of footmen in the upper gallery, a stray country cousin or two scattered throughout the theatre, and the picture of the audience is complete." (Nicoll, *Restoration Drama*, p. 8.)

morality. We need look for verification no further than the comedies of Dryden, that most illustrious of hack playwrights, whose characters, as Mr. Knights remarks of Etherege's Dorimant, are engaged in "intrigues of no more human significance than those of a barn-yard cock." [10] There are, nevertheless, exceptions in both periods; and an age—of drama or of any other genre—is to be judged, ultimately, by its masterpieces. *The Country Wife* is, as Mr. Knights says of Restoration comedy generally, "in the matter of sexual relations . . . entirely dominated by a narrow set of conventions." We have in it the fixed focus on the sex-pursuit, the wits and would-be wits exercising themselves on the pleasures of variety and the pains of marriage, the neglected and yearning wives, the jealous husband fearing cuckoldry and the foolish one inviting it, but no marriage—in this view of wives as damageable possessions—proof against it. The question whether Wycherley yields to and exploits these conventions, or examines and substantiates them, is left to be considered.

Volpone's pretense of mortal illness, which alerts every acquaintance persuaded of being his sole heir, is Jonson's device for drawing out and illuminating the unity of avarice, the reduction and dehumanizing of appetite, in the specious diversity of a society for which money has become its own justification.[11] Wycherley's device, within the conventions of his own stage and society, is equally brilliant: the rake Horner, to lull the suspicion of husbands and to secure in time the devotion of

10 Knights, *Explorations*, p. 158.

11 The society Jonson writes about is documented at length in Knights, *Drama and Society in the Age of Jonson* (London, 1937).

wives whose only coyness is for reputation's sake, pretends to have been made a eunuch and to be therefore no longer dangerous to either. Jonson's speaking rapacities, drawn out by his device, are obsessed by money, Wycherley's by sex; and Wycherley is no more the defender or dupe of the obsession he treats than is Jonson of his. As in Jonson, everything is expressed directly, in a transparent idiom, through which communication is both easy and impossible: Horner and Harcourt—the two manipulators—say what they mean and take care, when necessary, to be misunderstood; their dupes—Sparkish, Sir Jasper and his "ladies" —give themselves away in every phrase with no such intention at all; Alithea, saying what she means and intending to be taken at her word, is not believed especially when she is most earnest; Pinchwife, the cuckold in spite of himself, says what he means and, since his words mean more than he guesses, is understood in ways that must at last confirm his ferocious cynicism; only the country wife, like a judgment on this murk of rutting deceptions, says what she means with such country candor and naïveté as to clear the air from time to time, until she learns, having lost her lover, to lie habitually and for the sake of comfort with her husband: "And I must be a country wife still too, I find; for I can't, like a city one, be rid of my husband, and do what I list."

Standards become private and narcissistic, masquerading behind words once susceptible to public definition: honor, for example. For Pinchwife, honor is the patrolling of his "freehold," the banner of anticuckoldism. For Sparkish, it is the modish reflex against such insults as he is competent to unriddle. For Lady Fidget, it is a vacuum, the absence of scandal—"'tis not an injury to a husband, till it be an injury to our honours; so that a woman of honour loses no honour with a private person." For her husband it is the proper filling of social rôles in savorless private lives, as when he tells his wife to "go to your business, I say, pleasure, whilst I go to my pleasure, business," and sends her off to play games with that unscandalous shadow of a man, Horner. For Alithea, honor is stubbornness of fidelity to a detestable commitment, the sort of honor that sentimental comedy will take in dead earnest during Wycherley's own lifetime. Only for Horner, the sardonic, privileged observer, like Shakespeare's Diomede making his opportunities in a corrupt age without giving up a certain hard clarity of vision, is honor significantly honorable, the saving (for his own honorless aims) of his mistresses' reputations, which is all they wish saved, until, forced to choose between the "honor" of a concealed mistress and harmless Alithea's, he chooses his pleasure and must submit to Alithea's wistful reproach: "I always took you for a man of honour."

The dialogue is, throughout, a great web of ambiguities and unexpected, symbolic relevances: firecracker strings of *double-entendre* as in the china scene, intentions and words at cross-purposes and exposing each other, unconscious prophecies by gulls of their inevitable gulling, the insidious slipperiness of language in a society alerted to sex only. And the ambiguities are never merely stock comic devices in set-piece scenes and episodes, they are the confusions to which mind makes itself liable by reducing itself to caricature, by converting language into an unintentionally rich symbolism of aborted single impulse, such as flows over in the grotesque drinking scene between Horner

and the ladies: "The filthy toads," says Mrs. Dainty—she is talking about men—"choose mistresses now as they do stuffs, for
having been fancied and worn by others"; "For being common
and cheap," adds Mrs. Squeamish; "Whilst women of quality,"
concludes Lady Fidget, "like the richest stuffs, lie untumbled,
and unasked for."

This is the age of Nell Gwyn and the Duchess of Cleveland.
"Is it not a frank age?" Sparkish the ape of fashion asks rhetor-
ically, having just misinterpreted to his own satisfaction—as
civility, as wit, as up-to-dateness or upside-downness—a rival's
insults to him and declarations of love, over her protest, to the
girl he is to marry. "Blame 'em not, they must follow their copy,
the age," says one of Horner's friends about poets who create
fashionable fools. Frankness, somehow, is not enough. Nor is
monomaniacal vigilance: "What a swarm of cuckolds and cuck-
old-makers!" cries Pinchwife, preparing to assist with tenacious
(if unintended) complaisance at his own cuckolding; and, having
dictated to his wife her letter of disavowal for which she substitutes her own breathless solicitation, directs her to "write on
the backside, 'For Mr. Horner,'" and delivers it up—wife and
all—himself. Heroism is not enough: "I will not be a cuckold,"
says Pinchwife, "there will be danger in making me a cuckold";
and Horner punctures that bubble, "Why, wert thou not well
cured of thy last clap?"

Wycherley's toughmindedness, like Jonson's, is likely to repel
tender critics. "There can be no question," remarks one of the
recent admirers of Restoration comedy, "but that Wycherley is
indescribably vulgar." [12] Another will not admit him to the

[12] Nicoll, *British Drama* (4th ed., London, 1947), p. 252.

suave and truly comic company of Etherege and Congreve because

> Social folly and hypocrisy are much closer realities to . . .
> [him] than the social poise and integrity which make
> amends. . . . When other writers of Restoration comedy
> ridicule folly and vice, it is more lightheartedly and rarely
> with corrective emphasis. . . . On some occasions, Wych-
> erley assails some of the most cherished ideals of the age.
> . . . At such times . . . [he] is playing false to the tradi-
> tion of Restoration comedy of manners; he confirms our sus-
> picion that he was not 'born' a Restoration gentleman.[13]

The view that comedy is necessarily "lighthearted," gentlemanly, and careful of the "ideals of the age" would of course
have startled comic dramatists from Aristophanes to Jonson;
chiefly responsible, perhaps, for a view so vapidly genteel and,
since Meredith, so nearly axiomatic are the false example of
Shakespeare and the sentimental comedy that has dominated
the English stage since 1700. Nor does the term "comedy of manners" brighten and rarefy the comic atmosphere so much as all
that. A comic dramatist must use the materials his audience
affords him: the period during which the surface and finish of
life, wit and social adeptness monopolized the audience's image
of life produced as its characteristic genre the comedy of manners; just as in a period of more diversified interests Jonson, con-
centrating on a single possible Elizabethan image of life—life
as energy and appetite—produced the comedy of humors. But
to treat an image of life is not necessarily to defend or suppress

[13] Lynch, *The Social Mode*, pp. 173 ff.

its defects. Wycherley merely had less faith than his audience in the durability of manners and in their power to withstand the pressure of impulse or self-interest. The author has his rights also.

Still, to wince at Wycherley is more reasonable than to find in Congreve a prevailing "joyousness" and the portrait of a *"beau monde . . .* indulgently idealized"; [14] and this traditional view of *The Way of the World* particularly, as the prop and casual glory of Restoration society (or rather of its ghost), as an elegantly falsified testament dedicated by the age to itself, has long served both addicts and detractors of Restoration comedy, who unite in affirming that the comedy of manners can breathe only in an "air of modish triviality." [15]

Congreve, it is true, presents a society of superficies, in which manners are second nature and, therefore, distinctions of a primary nature—moral and psychological—are difficult to make. In the great world Fainall is scarcely distinguishable from Mirabell, and the false wits—snappers-up of considered trifles— scarcely distinguishable from the true ones. Both Fainall and Mirabell are witty and languidly polite, and the false wits can learn patterns of politeness and patterns of wit from such formal and artificial instructors. Manners are, or appear to be, opaque and durable, a common film of plausibility over the variety of impulse and motive.

Taken by itself, the entire first act of *The Way of the World* is a surface of ease and plausibility, barely ruffled even by the need to appear witty and detached. One is untempted, for ex- ample, to penetrate, so long as it occupies the stage, the rehearsed,

[14] *Ibid.,* p. 213.   [15] Nicoll, *British Drama,* p. 255.

serpentine elegance with which Fainall and Mirabell discuss women, courtship and marriage:

> She once used me with that insolence [says Mirabell, remembering Millamant] that in revenge I took her to pieces, sifted her, and separated her failings; I studied 'em, and got 'em by rote. The catalogue was so large that I was not without hopes one day or other to hate her heartily; to which end I so used myself to think of 'em at length, contrary to my design and expectation, they gave me every hour less and less disturbance; till in a few days it became habitual to me to remember 'em without being displeased. They are now grown as familiar to me as my own frailties; and in all probability, in a little time longer I shall like 'em as well.

"Marry her, marry her!" says Fainall. "Be half as well acquainted with her charms as you are with her defects, and my life on't, you are your own man again. . . . I have experience; I have a wife, and so forth." Later, Witwoud stumbles into these verbal dexterities with a compliment: "No man in town lives well with a wife but Fainall. Your judgment, Mirabell?" And Mirabell replies: "You had better step and ask his wife, if you would be credibly informed."

Manners—assembling themselves in the phrases so neatly pieced and developed, seeming to repel attention except to themselves—will very shortly, however, clear into a disquieting transparency: Mirabell *is* anxiously in love and incapable of rationalizing his way out of it; Fainall *has* learned from his own calculatedly loveless marriage and his secret affair that experience is a murderer of illusions; Mrs. Fainall, when she is asked, offers

a great deal of personal information, if only later the fact that
her lover, as well as the pander for her hateful marriage, was
Mirabell himself.

> Men are ever in extremes, either doting or averse. While
> they are lovers, if they have fire and sense, their jealousies are
> insupportable. And when they cease to love, (we ought to
> think at least) they loathe; they look upon us with horror
> and distaste, they meet us like the ghosts of what we were,
> and as from such, fly from us.

"You hate mankind?" asks Mrs. Marwood. "Heartily, inveter-
ately." "Your husband?" asks Mrs. Marwood. "Most transcendently; aye, though I say it, meritoriously." Mrs. Marwood, loving Mirabell without hope, trapped by Fainall in an affair from
which she has long since withdrawn any love of her own, can
at least amuse herself while she awaits the next occasion to crip-
ple Mirabell's hope of love and dowry both—inventing this bitter catechism for rejected ladies to live by.

The astonishing fact about the dialogue of *The Way of the
World* is not that it gives an immortal voice to the transience
of manners—as indeed it does—but that it expresses, with its
own imperturbable logic, a pervasive sophistication stifling all
vitality except fury, jealousy, cunning, affectation, contempt, and
perhaps the dignified uneasiness that occasionally breaks through
Mirabell's façade. Manners have tortured the characters, and
their language, into the substance as well as the style of self-
baffling intricacy. There is never even the sense—as there always
is in *The Country Wife*—of imminent sexual explosion: impulse
and motive have suffered alchemical changes; personality has

been, for the aims of the drawing-room, subtilized into a sleek, complacent uniformity; sex and self-interest and the need to sustain a perilous façade are all dissolved into one another. Charm at its best is the carefully poised, self-protective affectation of Millamant, scoring off Mrs. Marwood who has just insisted that she hates Mirabell:

> O madam, why so do I. And yet the creature loves me, ha! ha! ha! How can one forbear laughing to think of it! I am a sibyl if I am not amazed to think what he can see in me. I'll take my death, I think you are handsomer and, within a year or two as young; if you could but stay for me, I should overtake you, but that cannot be. . . .

In such a world, affectation may be the only armor. Cuckoldry and cozening, and the rigors of labyrinthine intrigue, are the way of this world, which is Fainall's world and Mrs. Marwood's; and Fainall is ultimately privileged to describe himself, in a corrosive shower of wit, as the blindest and most emblematic dupe of all:

> And I, it seems, am a husband, a rank husband; and my wife a very errant, rank wife, all in *the way of the world*. 'Sdeath, to be a cuckold by anticipation, a cuckold in embryo! Sure I was born with budding antlers, like a young satyr, or a citizen's child. 'Sdeath! to be out-witted, to be out-jilted, out-matrimonied! If I had kept my speed like a stag, 'twere somewhat; but to crawl after, with my horns, like a snail, and be outstripped by my wife, 'tis scurvy wedlock.

The comedy of manners does not necessarily trifle; it is hospitable to serious issues. It has for its subject, after all, the cult of manners that grandly offers to regulate a whole society, and the Arnoldian predisposition of Mr. Knights ought to have led him to scrutinize more patiently that cultivated appearance of triviality which Congreve, for one, accepts from his audience, and which he polishes into an ironic gloss not quite dazzling enough to conceal the moral turbulence beneath.

It is by now safe to assert that Sheridan, on the other hand, had a passive audience and no cult of manners; that this audience, bottle-fed on sermons and sentimental comedy, refused to recognize entire continents of vitality; that sex was inadmissible and irony incomprehensible; that good nature—which tended to be defined, dramatically, as an incapacity for thought—had replaced good manners; that Sheridan, the presumptive inheritor of the tradition of Congreve, found his inheritance dissipated before he could lay his hands on it, and was in fact writing, not comedies of manners, but—patched out with hasty reconstructions of Jonsonian and Restoration types—good-natured sentimental dramas of comic intrigue and situation, which Fielding had acclimated to fiction, in the guise of anti-sentimentalism, a generation before.

It may be that *The School for Scandal* is a better play than *The Rivals;* but both are miscellanies of stagey, actable situations incorporating sentimental and stock-comic types, and the former is, characteristically, indifferent enough toward motive and design to leave the scandalmongers of the title without function or effect in the play. *The Rivals,* in any case, is not much worse; and it is a more candid and melancholy epitaph on the comedy of manners, indeed on the English comic drama.

The most obvious quality of *The Rivals* is its literariness: its remoteness from live situations seen and live conversations recorded; its dependence on formula, contrivance, tips to the audience, plot summaries, scene-shifting and stage-business, playable circumstances and playable characters at the expense of consistency and subtlety, the comfortable simplifying echo of dead authors' perceptions—all the paraphernalia of the well-made popular play of any age.

Sheridan falls back on formula even while he affects to attack it. The sitting duck of the play is the Julia-Faulkland relationship; but its embarrassing woodenness will exceed the expectations of the most ill-disposed critic. Faulkland is ostensibly a satire on the sentimental hero of the novels Lydia borrows from the lending libraries—all nerves, doubt, sophistry, and remorse. Unluckily, however, he is presented at such length and with such abundant self-justification that Sheridan seems to be soliciting sympathy, or at least fatiguing our attention, on behalf of as windy a bore as any sentimental novel offers. And Julia, whom Sheridan exerts himself to contrast approvingly with her lover, is as smug and dreary a copybook of eighteenth-century posies as might be culled from the collected works of Charlotte Lennox:

> My heart has long known no other guardian—I now entrust my person to your honour—we will fly together. When safe from pursuit, my father's will may be fulfilled—and I

receive a legal claim to be the partner of your sorrows and tenderest comforter. Then on the bosom of your wedded Julia, you may lull your keen regret to slumbering, while virtuous love, with a cherub's hand, shall smooth the brow of upbraiding thought, and pluck the thorn from compunction.

To return from this preening flaccidity to any remark, however casual, by any of the women in *The Way of the World* is to measure interplanetary distances. Nor is Sheridan more successful when he attempts to manufacture—as a foil to Julia, that sober and responsible heroine—an up-to-date Millamant, her head turned by the reading of novels. The affectation of Congreve's Millamant has a purpose and is subordinated to her wit; the best Sheridan can do by way of expressing Lydia's affectation is to preface her otherwise characterless remarks with a "Heigh-ho!" and to feed the audience on curiously mixed, interminable catalogues of lending-library fiction, in which Smollett is equated with Sterne and both with the true-romance writers of the time—as if Sheridan, acquiescing in the eighteenth-century snobbery toward the novel, is himself incapable of making the distinctions. (One is reduced to looking for signs of the *author's* personality when he gives us no impression of personality, motive, or value in his characters.)

Even Sheridan's theatrical machinery makes alarming noises. In the opening scene two servants labor, during an implausibly crammed and hearty chat, to identify in detail all the characters and relationships of the play. The audience, as it doubtless deserves, is occasionally treated like an idiot with an ear trumpet:

"Ye powers of impudence, befriend me!" says Absolute in an aside, preparing to be impudent, or, preparing to act repentant, "Now for a penitential face"; and, fearful that we may not deduce the magnitude of Lydia's silliness from the incompetence of its presentation, he nudges us with bogus good humor—"Ha! ha! ha! one would think now that I might throw off all disguise at once, and seize my prize with security; but such is Lydia's caprice, that to undeceive were probably to lose her."

Conventions are not to be trusted, either. Setting up his recognition scene, in which Lydia looks forward to the prompt exposure of a deception that has in fact been practised only on her, Sheridan has Lydia turn her face from the door and keep it turned away through half the scene, while she wonders why "I han't heard my aunt exclaim yet! . . . perhaps their regimentals are alike, and she is something blind," and later, "How strangely blind my aunt must be!" The suspense is not in the dramatic use of a frankly theatrical device—to throw light, for example, on the cumulative extravagance of self-deception—but simply in waiting for Lydia, whose turning away has made the scene possible if not credible, to turn round and see what is there. Sheridan is working, here as elsewhere, not with live conventions but with stage tricks only.

The only figures Sheridan enjoys are his bullies and blusterers: Sir Anthony, the comic-tyrannical father; Acres, the good-natured, swearing country squire with an aversion to dying; Sir Lucius, the obsessed and doctrinaire duelist—"Pray, sir, be easy; the quarrel is a very pretty quarrel as it stands; we should only spoil it by trying to explain it." They are the only characters who speak with an approximation of personality, and they do their amusing vaudeville stunts with a verve that recalls to us, by unhappy contrast, the nullities in the leading rôles.

If Mrs. Malaprop is less consistently amusing (and she does have one Miltonic simile: "as headstrong as an allegory on the banks of Nile"), it is because her "nice derangement of epitaphs" is an unfunctional, isolated humor, usually a rambling collection of improbable errors interrupted by plain sense whenever Sheridan is anxious to advance the plot, and not at all a determined flood of self-revelation as with her great predecessor, Fielding's Mrs. Slipslop. Again, though, the shattering comparison is with Congreve, with the impressionable virago of an aunt that Sheridan found in *The Way of the World:* Lady Wishfort and her fishwife eloquence as, for example, when she casts off her scheming maid:

> Away! out! out! Go set up for yourself again! Do, drive a trade, do, with your three-pennyworth of small ware flaunting upon a packthread, under a brandy-seller's bulk, or against a dead wall by a ballad-monger! Go, hang out an old frisoneer-gorget, with a yard of yellow colberteen again. Do; an old gnawed mask, two rows of pins, and a child's fiddle; a glass necklace with the beads broken, and a quilted nightcap with one ear. Go, go, drive a trade! These were your commodities, you treacherous trull! . . .

It is not merely that Lady Wishfort is here speaking with a freedom rather indecorous for Sheridan's stage, but that she speaks always as a character involved in the action, and with an energy and particularity of vision beyond Sheridan's powers entirely.

We must pay our respects, eventually, to talent, for literary history cannot quite conjure it away. There is little enough talent in any age: the run of Restoration comic dramatists, working unimpeded before the same audience and in the same tradition as Wycherley, produced libraries of triviality, dullness, and smut. On the other hand, less satisfactory traditions—the Wordsworthian ruminative blank verse of the nineteenth century, for example—if they inhibit, do not necessarily prevent the operation of talent. Sheridan—after one has deplored his audience and the sentimental tradition it venerates and imposes—remains a second-rate and second-hand playwright: that there is no great playwright in his time may be the fault of the time, but Sheridan himself will have to bear some of the responsibility for being no better than he is.

Without a satisfactory tradition, the dramatist is, indeed, liable to be—of all artists—the most personal and most exhibitionistic failure, to overlook even such exploitable types and situations as Sheridan salvaged, to make unguided excursions into bathos, to mistake self-indulgence for originality and nose-thumbing for wit. Wilde, like Sheridan, is vaguely credited with having revived, for his time, the comedy of manners; but Wilde's *fin de siècle* was too remote from any comic tradition at all to allow him even such tag-ends of tradition as Sheridan's. In one sense, it is true, Wilde is far more than Sheridan a dramatist of manners: he does treat—in *The Importance of Being Earnest,* at least—a uniform and polished social surface. But it is a surface that he invents without the collusion of his audience, a fable of a society; and he is not enough of a fabulist to discover or invent the values that must prop or undermine it.

The best Wilde can do is to put his trust in the patterns and moral implications of epigram, or rather of a very limited and identifiable trick of epigram. He can do much worse, also; as in *Lady Windermere's Fan,* that incredible spectacle in which Wilde indecently embraces, in the presence of epigram, every Victorian cliché about wicked men, virtuous young women, self-sacrifice, and mother-love. When Cecil Graham ("lighting a cigarette") remarks, "I never seem to meet any but good women. The world is perfectly packed with good women. To know them is a middle-class education," Lord Darlington retorts, "This woman has purity and innocence. She has everything we men have lost": and before we are finished we have been lathered with Wilde's drama-school stage directions (*"Hiding her feelings with a trivial laugh,"* or *"Tears letter open and reads it, then sinks down into a chair with a gesture of anguish,"* or *"In her accents there is a note of deep tragedy. For a moment she reveals herself"*); we have been agitated by imminent disclosures to a young wife whose lackwit idealism is vulnerable, apparently, only to fact; we have been squeezed through wringers of remorse ("Why do I remember now the one moment of my life I most wish to forget? Does life repeat its tragedies? . . . Oh, how terrible! The same words that twenty years ago I wrote to her father! . . ."); and, having been purified in the self-immolation of a not quite unregenerate female heart, we rest in the stainlessness of Lady Windermere, fortifying herself with the "miniature she kisses every night before she prays" because

—as she tells Mrs. Erlynne, who, though Lady Windermere must never know, is really her mother!—"We all have ideals in life. At least we all should have. Mine is my mother." Mrs. Erlynne departs at last with the fan, a photo of her daughter and grandson, and a new husband; and Lady Windermere, saved, says to Lord Windermere: "I will trust you absolutely. Let us go to Selby. In the Rose Garden at Selby, the roses are white and red."

So automatic and superficial an epigrammatist as Wilde is, of course, mortally susceptible to the most pervasive sentimental currents of his time, since these flow at a level—in his audience, and in the cynicism he himself affects—to which his wit never penetrates. Beneath the epigrams is melodrama; and we must be grateful that, in *The Importance of Being Earnest,* Wilde never breaks the skin of artifice, of manners and wit in a fabulously idle society.

The Importance of Being Earnest is a formed play: in plot, characterization, relationship, incident, and language, it is as consistently and deliberately artificial as drama can be without forfeiting all human relevance. The outrageous formality gravely imposes itself, like a clown's top hat and spats, on the inconsequence of the fable. Everything is automatically classified in terms of everything else: an apparent jumble of names and haphazard connections that will fly accurately into predetermined position at the touch of a button; impartial attention to town life and country life so that both may be seen to take place, essentially, in drawing-rooms and full-dress; a pair of heroines who are twins of innocuous forthright response (to proposals, for instance: "What wonderfully blue eyes you have, Ernest! They are quite, quite blue," says Gwendolen; and "You dear romantic boy," says Cecily, "I hope your hair curls naturally, does it?"); two heroes, one making epigrams and the other pained by them, the latter turning out to be not only the brother but the older brother of the former; a social dragon whose guardianship of caste will not permit her to accept, socially, at least one sort of family background ("To be born, or at any rate bred, in a hand-bag, whether it had handles or not, seems to me to display a contempt for the ordinary decencies of family life that reminds one of the worst excesses of the French Revolution"); a celibate rector exchanging metaphors with a spinster governess —"Were I fortunate enough to be Miss Prism's pupil, I would hang upon her lips. (MISS PRISM *glares*.) I spoke metaphorically.—My metaphor was drawn from bees"; and Miss Prism's retaliation: "Ripeness can be trusted. Young women are green. (DR. CHASUBLE *starts*.) I spoke horticulturally. My metaphor was drawn from fruits."

Sex is admissible only through an inadvertence of imagery, and only then in small talk between an old maid and a parson. Manners can no longer be anything but trivial because the motives that could insist on their vitality have been banished from polite society; and Wilde is bold enough to make a virtue of triviality. Algernon begins the play with a considerable fuss about cucumber sandwiches; Lady Bracknell, having visited her recently widowed friend, observes that she has had "some crumpets with Lady Harbury, who seems to me to be living entirely for pleasure now"; Algernon is always hungry, and closes the second act eating muffins (". . . when I am in really great trouble, as anyone who knows me intimately will tell you, I refuse everything except food and drink"): the only mentionable im-

pulse is tea-party hunger, and the greatest mentionable pleasure
—which becomes the greatest imaginable—is tea-party eating.

The Importance of Being Earnest is, in any case, a sport—
triviality is a limited subject—and, admiring Wilde's achievement, we are likely to be unduly impressed by its almost parthe-
nogenetic isolation as well as by its unrepeatability. The real
trouble is that Wilde, on his own, performing before an audience
of cucumber sandwiches, unassisted by even Sheridan's eighteenth-
century rummage of sure-fire scenes and stereotypes, must rely
exclusively on his own wit to keep things together and moving;
and it will not stand the strain.

The trick of Wilde's epigram is, of course, to invert or dis-
tort commonplace; and occasionally it works. Lady Bracknell,
after her call on Lady Harbury for the first time "since her poor
husband's death," remarks, "I never saw a woman so altered;
she looks quite twenty years younger." Cecily says with her most
disarming pedantry: "It is always painful to part from people
whom one has known for a very brief space of time." But Wilde's
wit tends to exhaust itself in the manufacture of detachable epigrams, which—so he must hope, at least—will somehow, by standing with such conspicuous unanimity on their heads, arrange
themselves into formations of impudent comment on the manners and morals of upright society. Wilde's characteristic epigram,
and not only in *The Importance of Being Earnest,* is a puerile
tripping-up and dislocation of truism, especially about marriage:
"Girls never marry the men they flirt with"; "Divorces are made
in heaven"; "In marriage three is company and two is none";
"No married man is ever attractive except to his wife." Eventually Wilde himself becomes sufficiently aware of the porousness

of his wit to deny openly, in self-defense, the solid ground of genuine wit. "All women become like their mothers," says Algernon. "That is their tragedy. No man does. That's his." "Is that clever?" asks Jack; and Algernon makes a point of his pointlessness: "It is perfectly phrased! and quite as true as any observation in civilized life should be." One can even deny, finally, the utility of language. "I love scrapes," says Algernon. "They are the only things that are never serious." "Oh, that's nonsense, Algy," says straight-man Jack. "You never talk anything but nonsense." Algernon has an answer for that too, and it sounds like Wilde's own desperate answer: "Nobody ever does."

The Restoration comic dramatists had the advantage of the last English audience; and it was an accomplished audience, for whom manners were graces, and wit an exercise of the mind upon things in the world. Talking into the dark, one learns—as Wilde learned—to talk to oneself, and at length ceases to believe in talk altogether except as a kind of cheerless whistling. Laughter becomes more and more improbable, because there is no longer anything substantial to laugh at; and the comic dramatist—deprived of audience, deprived of subject and motive, deprived of any acceptable ideal of manners and decorum, deprived of everything but his own wit whirling in a void—has gone as far as possible toward writing for nobody about nothing at all.

Katherine Haynes Gatch

₰ THE LAST PLAYS OF BERNARD SHAW:
DIALECTIC AND DESPAIR

The low esteem in which Shaw's last plays are held when they are compared with those of his prime may in the long view be justified, but their reputation is in some measure the result of a failure to establish the critical bases on which these plays may be assessed as Shaw's peculiar contribution to English stage comedy in the second quarter of this century. That Shaw himself termed *Heartbreak House,* written on the eve of the First World War, "the most extraordinary" of his plays challenges his critics to examine closely the later comedies, which go still further in attempting new modes for an era that Shaw said made democracy "a fantasy acted by people in a dream." *Heartbreak House* Shaw had subtitled *A Fantasia in the Russian Manner on English Themes; The Apple Cart* (1929) he called *A Political Extravaganza.* The implication is strong that he had felt compelled to invent a genre to suit the inevitably political themes and the distorted human values of the world between two wars. To capture his vision of terrifying possibilities, Shaw, like other modern artists, relied on extravagance of manner and an atmosphere that sometimes suggests the absurdity of dreams.

The revival of *The Apple Cart* for the coronation year, 1953, indicates some of the misconceptions of Shaw's artistic and political premises still persisting at the mid-century. If this play is interpreted as praising monarchy in the person of King Magnus, then *The Apple Cart,* like *Candida* and *Saint Joan,* enjoys popular success for quite un-Shavian reasons. Actually, Shaw is using the king only as his symbol for the supreme aristocrat in the classic sense of the person best fitted to rule because he has been disciplined for public office and is willing to undertake its responsibilities with "the high republican conscience." *The Apple Cart* makes political the ironic pattern that Shaw had acknowledged a generation earlier as basic to his work. "I deal," he said, "in the tragi-comic irony of the conflict between real life and the romantic imagination. . . ." The grotesque spectacle of real life after 1918 required a tonality very different from that of the comedies written in the traditions of Shakespeare, of Molière, and even of Ibsen. Yet Shaw did not, like some artists in this age, go so far as to disintegrate the inherited techniques of his craft, because to the last he hoped that the meaningless fragmentation of democratic society was not the promised end. Hope and belief gave Shaw his dramatic structure, but in the last plays fear and disgust created the tone; and where hope wavers, the structure is weak.

The most tiresome commonplace in the criticism of Shaw's plays, early and late, is that they are all talk and no plot. Why, if these plays are not plays, should they behave on the stage as if they were? The question is not answered by saying that Shaw, while avowing his debt to the comedy of manners, cunningly concealed it by inverting the conflicts and resolutions of that comedy to make his conversation pieces viable for the stage. Chesterton early pointed out the crucial importance of "conversion" in the typical Shavian story; Edmund Wilson declared but did not demonstrate that the Marxian analysis of society gave the plays structure; Eric Bentley has mentioned dialectic and warned critics to watch for the "synthesis" in the working out of Shaw's comic situations, illustrating his meaning of synthesis in a valuable commentary on *Major Barbara*.

I wish to suggest that Shaw often used a dialectical structure derived from Hegel and Marx, but beguilingly modified by his own temperament, observations, and convictions. By dialectic, for want of a pleasanter term, I mean the tripartite pattern in which Hegel envisaged historical change and which Marx and Engels turned to their own uses: thesis, antithesis, and synthesis. It should be said at once that Shaw's use of the triad is not unrelated to his more personal and Socratic dialectic, the search for truth out of half-truths and differing opinion; but for the discussion of plot the dialectic process must be understood as divisible into three phases. The essence of the Hegelian dialectic is change, just as the essence of the Socratic dialectic is progression through contraries. Whatever the condition of a Shavian play, it is not static. Like Hegel and like Marx in their treatment of historical change, Shaw opens his comedies with a social situation temporarily well consolidated. Hegel's illustration was republican Rome; Marx's eye was fixed on the bourgeois society of his own century; and there too was Shaw's beginning. From within republican Rome (thesis) Caesar broke away (antithesis) and ultimately effected the synthesis of the empire. But where Hegel brought the process to rest in the Prussian state, and Marx could not seem to imagine anything beyond the classless society which he fancied would follow the revolution, Shaw as a Creative Evolutionist conceived of unending change. At the close of *Back to Methusaleh* Lilith says, "It is enough that there is a beyond."

The reading of Marx had awakened the young Shaw to the importance of the economic bases of society, but he could no more be a consistent dialectical materialist than he could as a Creative Evolutionist be a scientific determinist. The comic spirit is inimical to the rigid mental habits of the ideologue. Shavian laughter springs from the common sense that Bergson describes as "the mobility of the intelligence conforming exactly to the mobility of things . . . the moving continuity of our attention to life." The Shavian dialectic uses in its synthesis the solvent of the comic spirit and corrects both the Prussianism of Hegel and the proletarian ideology of Marx by the humanity of the great comic tradition.

When in 1897 Shaw, at the top of his form as a critic, reviewed Meredith's long-unpublished *Essay on Comedy and the Uses of the Comic Spirit,* he seized upon Meredith's thesis that comedy civilizes and responded gratefully to Meredith's praise of the masters of the comic spirit as an intellectual aristocracy. "Look there for your unchallengeable upper class," Meredith said. "He should know," Shaw commented, "for he certainly belongs to it." In Meredith, Shaw found his prophet. Disavowing any taste for Norwegian gloom, Shaw hinted that his own comedies, awaiting publication in the next year, would claim spiritual kinship with Shakespeare and Molière. In the very year in which Shaw praised Meredith's essay he created General Burgoyne of *The Devil's Disciple,* a brilliant aristocrat in the eighteenth-century manner, who personifies at once the spirit of comedy and Shaw's own temperament. Of him Shaw says in his notes to the play:

> Burgoyne . . . is a man who plays his part in life, and makes all his points, in the manner of a born high comedian. . . . His peculiar critical temperament and talent, artistic, satirical, rather histrionic, and his fastidious delicacy of sentiment, his fine spirit and humanity, were just the qualities to make him disliked by stupid people because of their dread of ironic criticism.

And one might add, these are just the qualities needed to modify the humorless excesses of the doctrinaire.

Certainly the heroes and heroines of Shavian comedy are for the most part the wellborn, readily articulate, and self-directing people of traditional high comedy. They serve as the antithetical agents when the dialectic operates in the plot, for Shaw trusted his observation that revolutionary leaders do not spring from the proletariat. A Barbara Undershaft (or a Beatrice Webb as Shaw had observed in real life) breaks away from the security of the ancestral mansion to carry salvation to the world of slums and dark satanic mills. Lady Cicely Waynefleet, with seemingly inconsequent charm, converts the dispossessed Captain Brassbound to her view that hatred and violence on his part will make him as bad as his oppressors, and cannot right the injustice done to his dead mother. John Tanner, author of "The Revolutionist's Handbook," confers on himself the degree MIRC—Member of the Idle Rich Class—and acknowledges his chauffeur, Henry Straker, as the new and unillusioned man. Vivie and Fanny are graduates of Cambridge. The Roman Lavinia, who leads the

martyrs to the arena for the god whom her free mind will not
let her name or localize, is a patrician with a fine scorn for the
irresponsible members of her class and deep pity for the op-
pressed. The aristocratic principle in Shavian comedy operates
in the critical intelligence, the cultivated sensibilities, and above
all in the acceptance of responsibility. In Shaw's late plays, as in
his early ones, these qualities of mind and character constitute
the hope for society. But in the late plays the hope that they
can be made to function politically is so deferred as to suggest
despair.

To make this aspect of the late plays clear it is necessary to consider a few early ones where by contrast the dialectic works
with precision and confidence. I am sorry to have to mention
Candida, but Shaw's only explicit statement about his use of
thesis and antithesis relates to that play and has been overlooked
by the Candidamaniacs:

> The time was ripe for a modern pre-Raphaelite play. Re-
> ligion was alive again, coming back upon men, even upon
> clergymen, with such power that not the Church of Eng-
> land itself could keep it out. . . . To distil the quintessential
> drama from pre-Raphaelitism, medieval or modern, it must
> be shewn at its best in conflict with the first broken, nervous,
> stumbling attempts to formulate its own revolt against itself
> as it develops into something higher. A coherent explana-
> tion of any such revolt . . . can only come when the work
> is done. . . .

The tell-tale phrases here are *revolt against itself* and *develops
into something higher.* Of Eugene Marchbanks and his conflict

with the Christian Socialist clergyman Morell, Shaw says point-
edly:

> Here, then, was the higher but vaguer and timider vision,
> the incoherent, mischievous, and even ridiculous unpractical-
> ness, which offered me a dramatic antagonist for the clear,
> bold, sure, sensible, benevolent, salutarily short-sighted Chris-
> tian Socialist idealism.

Obviously this is a statement of thesis and antithesis. Candida's
maiden name was Burgess. Christian Socialism is wedded to
and dependent upon bourgeois comfort. Significantly, although
Eugene, the wellborn, hates to see Candida peel onions, he hates
even worse to see her break Morell's spirit, for his instincts are
those of high breeding, and he recoils from cruelty. The synthesis—which is the secret in the playwright's heart—will fuse
Morell's Christianity, Candida's practicality, and Eugene's critical intelligence.

Major Barbara demonstrates the Shavian dialectic very clearly
and it is an invaluable aid to the understanding of the late plays.
Mr. Bentley is right, I think, in seeing its hero in Adolphus
Cusins, the professor of Greek. He is also right in thinking that
Undershaft is the false Nietzschean Superman who fancies himself beyond good and evil. The humorous and scholarly Cusins
nicknames Undershaft "Mephistopheles," calling attention to
the fact that like Goethe's antagonist he does good with evil intentions. I should like to place even greater emphasis on the
professor of Greek as the true protagonist. Not only does the
conclusion represent the synthesis of Barbara's love and faith
with her father's practical genius; Cusins functions as the

humanist whose knowledge of the past is needed to give right direction to the future. It is inexcusably literal minded to see the Undershaft gunpowder as anything but a symbol for power. You can't have power for good without risking power for evil, as Cusins says. The responsible intellect must control power, as it must also light the way for Barbara's faith, lest it become fanaticism. The aristocratic principle operates in Barbara, too, and she is both comically and heroically the noblewoman when, catching Cusins' vision, she cries:

> I have got rid of the bribe of bread. I have got rid of the bribe of heaven. Let God's work be done for its own sake: the work he had to create us to do because it cannot be done except by living men and women. When I die, let him be in my debt, not I in his; and let me forgive him as becomes a woman of my rank.

The dialectic is part of the joke in *Fanny's First Play*. The critics whom Fanny's father summons utter every cliché that has dogged Shaw's reputation, but they fail to understand the dynamics of the plot. The play presents two bourgeois households, both alike in dignity, long associated in business, and now about to be further consolidated by marriage. The houses of Gilbey and Knox are redolent of the atmosphere of the dissenting Protestant sects, which, according to one reading of history, aided capitalism in disintegrating the medieval synthesis. Bobby Gilbey is rebellious against the strictness of home and against the pietism of a Catholic tutor, who has been hired because his brother, a monsignor, is a customer of the family business. Bobby's marriage contract with Margaret Knox is threatened by his preference

for Dora Delany, daughter of joy and of the proletariat. After
a too joyful evening Dora lands herself and Bobby in jail for
disorderly conduct. Meanwhile, Margaret, on her way home from
an evangelistic meeting, with spirit set free, picks up a French
naval officer and goes dancing with him. In a police raid, Margaret,
like Bobby, goes to jail. The dialectical farce is brought to a hilarious synthesis when a way is found for a happy future by the
Gilbeys' monumental butler, Juggins, who reveals at the crisis
that he is the brother of a duke, and that he is doing penance by
servitude for having insulted a member of the working class. The
noble Juggins, heretofore useful only as arbiter of taste to the
bourgeoisie, will now be united with the group, for he has fallen
in love with Margaret Knox, who appeals more than ever to his
aristocratic tastes for having lost her middle-class conventionality
in Holloway Gaol. Bobby and Dora will complete the synthesis
in a classless society where "like will to like"—and the brother
of a duke will teach Dora table manners. The final Shavian
trademark is the moment of real feeling when Mrs. Knox, a sin-
cerely religious woman who understands both penitence and
joy, transfers her belief in conversion to a social context. *Fanny's
First Play* stands to Shaw's first plays in the self-critical relation
of *A Midsummer Night's Dream* to early Shakespearean comedy.
It demonstrates that Shaw's comic sense saved him from the rigidity of pattern.

After this *tour de force, Androcles and the Lion* begins a new
phase and looks toward the deepening moods of *Heartbreak
House* and *Saint Joan*. While *Major Barbara* treated sincere but
youthful religious enthusiasm with propriety in the atmosphere
of social comedy, *Androcles and the Lion,* where the odor of blood

rises from the arena, could preserve comic tone only by recourse to fantasy. The ridiculous Antonine Emperor marks the decline of Rome, but the truly antithetical force within the state, the force that can set Caesars at naught, is the Christian humility of Androcles and the blood of the martyrs, the seed of an organization mightier than Caesardom. Androcles and his lion go waltzing off together in symbolic synthesis. The lion, like the Undershaft gunpowder, is power, an authentic Christian symbol. The lion must be uncaged but controlled by Androcles. Counterpointed against the ineffable humility of Androcles is the intellectual integrity of Lavinia, whose patrician distinction of mind defines the values which Androcles and his lion must maintain. This is essentially the same synthesis as in *Major Barbara:* faith and power must be directed by responsible mind.

Heartbreak House is the hinge between Shaw's early and late plays and records crisis for the playwright as for the world. In Captain Shotover, Shaw grasped the exasperation of aging genius with the mass of "practical" men who will not take a disinterested view of human destiny. "There is enmity between our seed and their seed," says Shotover. ". . . When we believe in ourselves we shall kill them." To which Hector, with deeper humanity, replies, "It is the same seed. . . . We are members one of another." Long before, writing of *The Master Builder,* Shaw had commented on "the sublime delirium that sometimes precedes bodily death . . . and the horror that varies the splendor of delirium." His last plays may have been called extravaganzas because Shaw felt in his own art something of that delirium and of that horror. "Why should not old men be mad?"

After the war, the Hegelian reading of history was rendered

obsolete by the theories of Petrie and Spengler, which better suited the postwar temper. As a Creative Evolutionist, accustomed to the long view, Shaw easily adapted himself to the cyclical concept of history in *Back to Methuselah,* his first postwar play. But *The Tragedy of an Elderly Gentleman* and *Saint Joan* both bear witness to the emotional experience which separated the postwar Shaw from the hopeful Fabian who had once gaily adapted dialectic to comedy.

Too True to Be Good (1932), written when Shaw was almost as old as Captain Shotover and King Lear, reveals both his humanity toward a younger generation drowning in despair and his own desperate clinging to the raft of dialectic. Like *The Apple Cart,* this play is subtitled *A Political Extravaganza,* although it presents its meaning in terms of private lives rather than cabinet crises and puts its emphasis on the spiritual ills of the postwar world. The maladies are those incident to the children of nineteenth-century parents, and there are no simple remedies. In a new key of extravagant absurdity, Shaw enters a realm of multiple suggestion and complexity of mood, yet the three acts and their settings afford recognizable dialectic symbolism.

Act I opens in the fetid atmosphere of a sickroom where every window is sealed against fresh air and where lavish appointments intensify the feeling of bad ventilation. Clearly Shaw's disgust with the ill health of capitalist society is very different from the mood in which, a quarter of a century earlier, he had depicted the stodgy comfort of Lady Britomart Undershaft's drawing room. But the action, the revolt of a sick daughter from the career of invalidism which her managing mother has organized for her, parallels Barbara's flight from Mayfair to the work of the Salvation Army. Both young women have made "the revolt from within." In order that the extravaganza should at once establish itself as a dramatic type, the play opens with a fantasy of a monstrous microbe, possibly a warning to the literal minded that the play may make them quite, quite ill. To prevent this misfortune, the Theatre Guild persuaded Beatrice Lillie to play the role of Sweetie, the nurse, and encouraged her to steal the show. The Shavian action, however, involves the stealing of a necklace which belongs to the Patient. That unappetizing invalid is an unconscious fraud who needs only an object in life to enable her to spring from the bed, join the eloquent burglar, Aubrey Bagot, and the nurse who is his accomplice, in the theft of her own jewels, and take off with them for a spree in primitive places.

Escape from the sickroom takes the Patient, in the second act, into the unbearable glare of a sandy and tropical terrain, where the primitive is too suddenly substituted for the over-civilized. Beneath the absurd incidents, the substructure of the classic antithesis is visible in mock violence suggestive of the end of an era of imperialism. The trio find themselves involved with Colonel Tallboys, numskull and water-colorist, in charge of the military post, who provokes an attack from the native tribe by his total ignorance of the ways of the desert. All the Europeans owe their lives in the end to the common sense and common humanity of Private Meek—the character with more than a touch of genius who is likely to turn up in any typical Shavian comedy. The scenes involving Meek and Tallboys are lovely farce in Shaw's early manner, and Private Meek is Shaw's gay tribute to his friend Lawrence of Arabia, who by this time was calling himself T. E. Shaw. Meek's knowledge of dialects, his ingenuity and omnipresence, his motorcycle, his headgear, and his habit of demoting himself to the ranks are Lawrence to the life. The satire on the military mind of Tallboys, who aggravates the dangerous friction between the white and dark races, is integral to the scheme of this political extravaganza. The intellectual grasp of international relations, as Shaw understands it, amounts to common sense and humanity raised to the degree of genius in experts like Lawrence—but the numskulls and water-colorists remain in command.

The third act, which in strict accord with dialectic should effect a synthesis, is strangely set in a surrealistic waste land where we may make what we can of the narrow gap, the symbolic grottoes suggestive of outworn cultures, and the beach with its sand and stones. The atmosphere of this scene is a far cry from the shining efficiency of the Undershaft works and the model town of the last act of *Major Barbara*. As in that play, the high point of the last act is the intellectual clash between an older man, product of nineteenth-century philosophy, and a younger one. But whereas Adolphus Cusins and Andrew Undershaft find a way to work together, and a hopeful future lies before Barbara and her learned lover, in *Too True to Be Good* the clash is never resolved. Aubrey, the erstwhile burglar, and his father, who appears here as the Elder, denounce each other, and Aubrey and the Patient separate, he to be swallowed up in a fog of intellectual despair, the girl to find practical work.

Aubrey Bagot's father, the Elder, is a nineteenth-century atheist and scientific determinist from whose relentless moral sternness the boy had long since taken refuge in religion, getting himself ordained while at Oxford. During the war, Aubrey became an ace with a brilliant record for bombing civilians. In the morbidity of self-loathing afterward, he took up with Sweetie, the nurse, and completed his experiments in degradation by turning burglar. Sweetie is a promiscuous vulgarian who, on the expedition in the second act, masquerades as a countess. She is a Shavian inversion of the postwar women of high social position and promiscuous habits, like Lucy Tantamount of *Point Counter Point*. Aubrey attributes his despair and depravity to the determinism of his father, but he also resembles the intellectuals of the lost generation who under the tutelage of D. H. Lawrence discovered the mystique of the lower centers. Aubrey's relation to the nineteenth-century Elder, his twentieth-century associates, his return to religion, and his eloquent despair suggest that his real name was Aldous, that the Elder's name was Thomas, and that Shaw felt tragicomedy in the plight of both generations of Huxleys. For the Elder, Newton's universe, which was the "stronghold of rational Determinism . . . has crumbled like the walls of Jericho before the criticism of Einstein," and "the calculable world has become incalculable." The illusion of design in the universe which had been an esthetic substitute for theology now mocks the neo-Darwinian. When he goes to a museum of natural history he sees "nothing in those grotesque monsters of the deep but the caricatures of some freakish demon artist. . . ." Rushing out of the museum lest he go mad, and demanding a solid footing in dogma, he is made dizzier still by realizing that "the only trustworthy dogma is that there is no dogma." His son, brought up to be "an incorruptible God-fearing atheist," has become a scoundrelly religious burglar.

The Elder bids him go drown himself. At the end Aubrey holds the stage alone. As the others sneak away from his preaching, he says,

> They are too absurd to be believed in; yet they are not fictions: the newspapers are full of them: what storyteller . . . would dare to invent figures so improbable as men and women with their minds stripped naked? . . . The horror of the naked mind is still more than we can bear.

At this point, however, the critics of *Too True to Be Good* missed their cue. They leapt to the conclusion that Aubrey's despair was Shaw's despair and quoted maliciously:

> I am by nature and destiny a preacher. I am the new Ecclesiastes. But I have no Bible, no creed: the war has shot both out of my hands. . . . I am ignorant: I have lost my nerve; . . . all I know is that I must find the way of life, for myself and all of us, or we shall surely perish. And meanwhile my gift has possession of me: I must preach and preach and preach no matter how late the hour and how short the day, no matter whether I have nothing to say—

and the fog from the sea envelops him. That Shaw's critics crowed to find these signs of pessimism in him was perhaps the nemesis visited upon one who had used Macbeth's nihilism as evidence of Shakespeare's own philosophical bankruptcy. But Shaw could talk back to his critics. In one of the Malvern Festival programs he singled out Mr. Krutch for punishment:

> I find it hard to forgive him for saying that I announced, in . . . *Too True To Be Good,* that world affairs are now

irremediable, and that mankind is damned beyond hope and redemption. . . . The despair of the shell-shocked young gentleman-burglar-clergyman, who made such a pitiful attempt to be happy by spending a lump of unearned money, is not my despair. . . . I made him a good preacher to warn the world against mere fluency, and the result was that his talking took Mr. Krutch in. He must be more careful next time.

The eloquence which Shaw has always generously lent even to characters of whom he disapproved has often taken critics in. Aubrey's prototype is the Devil of *Man and Superman.* The clue to meaning lies always in the character who goes off at the end to *do* something. Here the recovered Patient is the hopeful case. Debilitating as her sickroom has been, the girl has standards. Though she learns to be frank in speech, her taste is offended by Sweetie. After a brief fling with Aubrey she is bored, and wants a good hard job of practical work to do. In the end she makes an amusing alliance with her mother. The old lady, Mrs. Mopley, has had a blow on her head from Colonel Tallboys for disturbing him at his water colors, and it does her good. Shaw may be indicating that the stupidity and brutality of the war knocked sense into many left-over Victorians. Mrs. Mopley fails to recognize her coddled and cosseted daughter in the bronzed and athletic Patient whom she really likes. Now, the awakened mother and the rebellious daughter go off together "to found a sisterhood of service, like St. Teresa, with the mother as cook-housekeeper." This alliance of energetic mother and daughter is faintly reminiscent of the rapprochement of Lady Britomart and Barbara on the housekeeping level. They

are perhaps the Intelligent Women for whom Shaw wrote the
Guide to Socialism and Capitalism in his despair at fallacious
argument among men.

The title of *On the Rocks* echoes Captain Shotover's warning
to irresponsibles as to the fate of the drifting ship; and twenty
years after *Heartbreak House* it seemed that the democracies
were indeed drifting onto the rocks of fascist or proletarian dic-
tatorship. The tone of *On the Rocks* is dread. Vestigial remains
of the dialectic are visible only in a eugenic farce, almost as
obvious as *Fanny's First Play*. The farce has to do with the
love affairs of the Prime Minister's children. His overbred son,
David, is to marry one Aloysia Brollikins, a bounding daughter
of the proletariat, winner of many scholarships and politically
more literate than the Prime Minister. Miss Brollikins comes
onto the scene with the working class delegation. Flavia, the
Prime Minister's daughter, who has yearned for the rough mas-
culinity of a working man, settles for a radical peer, the Earl
of Barking, fresh from Oxford. He is a strident tough in a turtle-
necked pullover, in which disguise he is expiating the sins of
class pride, like Juggins the butler in *Fanny's First Play*. Shaw
strikes off the emergent radical types of the thirties brilliantly,
but because they are ideological fanatics, he finds them thoroughly unlovely when compared with Barbara Undershaft and
her Oxford professor. In this play the dialectic is adventitious
farce.

The real meaning of *On the Rocks* inheres in the character
of Sir Arthur Chavender, the Prime Minister whose week-end
conversion to a radical philosophy satirizes political amateurs
during the depression. With the ship almost on the rocks the

gentleman amateur is not a figure of fun, and the hilarious Cabinet meetings here, as in *The Apple Cart,* are really appalling. The satire never deals so sharply with the Prime Minister, however, as by implication it deals with the audience who votes for him. Thirty years earlier Shaw had said, "What our voters are in the pit and gallery, they are in the polling booth." At the prescription of a fashionable lady psychiatrist, Chavender makes a Friday to Tuesday retreat, accompanied by volumes of Marxist literature instead of his customary detective stories and copy of Wordsworth. Returning from his retreat with the fresh ardor of the convert, he sets the politicians in an uproar by his proposals for radical change. Then, with his customary charm, he declines responsibility and resigns. But the farce evaporates from the last moments of the play when he explains to his wife why he is not the man for the job: "I shall hate the man who will carry it through for his cruelty and for the desolation he will bring on us and our like." This is one of those quick transitions to genuine feeling which everyone versed in Shavian comedy will recognize. The Chavender type, whose good will the early Fabians had hoped might be taken up into the new synthesis, has not acquired political acumen. The curtain falls on the sound of shattering glass and the singing of the unemployed, "England, arise! the long, long night is over"; but in ironic counterpoint comes the thwacking sound of police batons.

The real horror implied in the ending of *On the Rocks* is expressed in the formidable title of its preface, "Extermination." Critics have shuddered in alarm at this preface without seeing that it modulates from irony to direct appeal and back again without warning, in the manner of Swift. Had Shaw called it

"A Modest Proposal for the Extermination of the Politically Irresponsible," readers might have heard the overtone of the first subheading, "Killing as a Political Function." The opening paragraph ends with one of Swift's matter-of-fact sentences: "Extermination must be put on a scientific basis if it is ever to be carried out humanely and apologetically as well as thoroughly." The seeming approval of cold-blooded Russian methods is given the lie by the moving plea, in the later part, for the sacredness of criticism. "Beware," Shaw says, "how you kill a thought that is new to you." That anyone could read to the end of the preface and still not understand his intention is a risk that as professional ironist he must have been willing to take. Bernard Shaw could not, like the rigid Hegelian or Marxist, countenance cruelty. He balances his acceptance of historical necessity by an impassioned plea for tolerance—the political theme of *Saint Joan*. With a flash of his invincible faith in the future, he directly answers Yeats's despair in "The Second Coming" with a deft verbal echo of the horrendous beast slouching toward Bethlehem to be born. "The beast of prey," Shaw said, "is not striving to return: the kingdom of God is striving to come."

The theme which links *On the Rocks* to *The Simpleton of the Unexpected Isles* is the coming up to judgment of the irresponsibles. Edmund Wilson has called *The Simpleton* Shaw's only really silly play, and there is no denying the afflicting ineptitude of its allegory. Although Shaw may be credited with having intended *The Simpleton* to provoke a revulsion against silliness, this play must be counted an experiment that brought art to the vanishing point. *The Simpleton* closes with the suggestion that the future belongs to the learners and that western man is no longer capable of learning. A civilization rotten with illusions is judged and discarded. The survivors are an ambiguous pair of orientals. Significantly, there is no vestige of the dialectic. *The Simpleton of the Unexpected Isles* has no structure, and it conveys the feeling that the failure of this civilization is a farce of simple-minded folly, not a twilight of the gods.

In *The Millionairess* (1936) Shaw returned, with reservations, to the hopeful synthesis. The heroine has the galvanic energy that marked the conductors of the Life Force in the early comedies; but she is, in the words of the man she is about to marry against his will, "a terrible woman," and Shaw means it. The Egyptian doctor has explained quite clearly all the reasons for *not* renouncing the ascetic bachelorhood of his dedicated life, but as Epifania extends her wrist he automatically puts his finger on her pulse and takes out his watch. "You are a terrible woman . . . but I love your pulse and I cannot give it up." The Egyptian doctor represents the holy wisdom, which may or may not be garnered in the East, but which the West with its megalomanic energy certainly lacks. Epifania, the millionairess, has an unholy and appalling vitality, a pulse "like a slow sledge hammer," but she is mean, bullying, avaricious, and a law unto herself. She makes money by instinct and bosses everyone. I fear Shaw meant her for the United States of America. Although Katharine Hepburn in her recent revival of *The Millionairess* lacked the vitality to realize those terrifying energies, the play proved stageworthy, if only as farce. *The Millionairess* is actually a morality play, in which the doctor speaks the last word, warning that "the wrath of Allah shall overtake those who leave the world no better than they found it." Epifania, like the Undershaft symbol, is power. The hope is that the Egyptian doctor, an intellectual aristocrat, like the professor of Greek, will use power for good; for he accepts responsibility and is indifferent to personal success. He shares Barbara's dedication to service and its religious motivation, but not her humanity. In *The Millionairess,* the familiar Shavian dialectic takes on larger dimensions. The synthesis is no longer a fusion of classes. It is no less than the vision of one world in the union of East and West.

Geneva (1938), the play in which the farcical dictators, Battler, Bombardone, and Flanco, are summoned to a court of pure justice, shows a world synthesis to be very far off. The machinery for international cooperation is in the hands of superpatriots like Begonia Brown. Begonia, the proliferating plant of the suburbs, is passionately loyal to Camberwell, and has no conception of abstract justice. There is some faint hope for the world, however, because the nations answer the summons to court. Shaw was to write two more plays, *In Good King Charles' Golden Days,* on the eve of the Second World War, and *Buoyant Billions* after it was over. In *King Charles* he abandoned the dialectic to let the Merry Monarch look down the centuries to come and see a melancholy vista of conflict. In *Buoyant Billions,* the playwright in his nineties found hope only in mathematical abstraction and ended with the marriage of an heiress to a young man who will devote his life to research for the mathematical hormone.

In all Shaw's late plays the ironic relationship between the magnitude of the themes and the triviality of the treatment is calculated; the political extravaganzas are tragicomedies, concerned with the grotesque disproportion between the gigantic problems and the pygmies who deal with them. Thomas Mann has said:

> The striking feature of modern art is that it has ceased to recognize the categories of tragic and comic, or the dramatic classifications, tragedy and comedy. It sees life as tragicomedy, with the result that the grotesque is its most genuine style—to the extent, indeed, that today that is the only guise in which the sublime may appear. . . . The grotesque is the genuine anti-bourgeois style.[1]

Whatever the ultimate verdict about the artistic success of Shaw's late plays, as an aging man he was not unresponsive to the compulsions upon the artist to find new modes for our time.

[1] H. T. Lowe-Porter, trans., *Past Masters* (London, 1933), p. 240 (Mann's Preface to the German version of Conrad's *The Secret Agent*).

ᴥᶘ THE COMEDY OF T. S. ELIOT

Nobody, I suppose, outside of classical studies, any longer reads either of A. W. Verrall's delightfully systematic distortions of Euripides, those two engaging and outrageous books, *Four Plays of Euripides* and *Euripides the Rationalist*. Yet Verrall as a critic bears rereading, less for his rationalist hypothesis, which hopelessly trapped his perceptions, than for the acuteness of those perceptions and his lucid and suggestive wrongheadedness. Indeed, I sometimes suspect that the reason classicists, apart from their native dislike of novelty, have been slow to adopt the techniques of the New Criticism is that Verrall (along with Samuel Butler) parodied and abused them before they formally existed, and so put the classicists off for half a century.

I have myself no wish to put anyone off, not even to put the New Critics off with Verrall. My use here for Verrall is mainly cautionary: I once had the unhappy but common experience of out-Verralling Verrall on *The Cocktail Party,* and I have no wish to repeat that performance, even if I could muster the necessary ingenuity. But I also wish to discuss Euripides' dramatic structure in relation to Eliot's comedy in the hope of making the much greater dramatist illustrate the methods and also (what I take to be) the failure of the lesser. For, unless I am badly mistaken, Eliot's Christian New Comedy of conversion is structurally very close to the movement, though not the meaning, of Euripidean drama. And Verrall, on the crucial point, comes pat to the comparison.

Verrall's theory of Euripidean structure will be immediately intelligible to anyone who has read even a little of recent Melville criticism. It rests entirely on two perceptions, both of which seem to me indisputably accurate. First is what might be called Euripides' quarrel with the gods of Olympos, that transparent rationalism in the tradition of Xenophanes that makes him surround such myths as Leda's egg or Thyestes' feast with a dubious "so men say" or "the story goes"; or, even more strongly, his outright assertion that the *logoi* of the Homeric gods are "the wretched tales of poets." Second, Verrall noticed that in play after play there comes a point where the literal action as dramatized cannot be accepted without gross inconsistency or intolerable paradox; the play appears to say one thing and to dramatize it as real, and then to assert somehow an antithetical reality. Thus in the *Herakles,* for instance, the hero is shown suffering madness as the result of the direct intervention of the goddess Hera's agents, Iris and Madness herself; yet later in same play Herakles boldly asserts a principle whose apparent consequence is the denial of the reality of the experience out of which the assertion is made in the first place. Herakles, that is, simply denies that the actions of the gods could in fact be such as they have been dramatized to be.

On the basis of these two perceptions, and this suggestion of a double pattern of reality in the plays, Verrall inferred that two simultaneous actions were being presented on two simul-

taneous "levels": the superficial action was "ostensible" and
the profounder action was "real." By an ostensible plot Verrall meant one so constructed as to give no offense to the vulgar and pious when dealing with received religious traditions,
an action which presented "things as they are said to be," *as if*
they were real, while the real action was a human story entirely
divested of the improbable or fabulous. In order to provide this
double plot with a double audience, Verrall assumed an elite of
sophoi, rationalist intellectuals who would see through the ostensible absurdities and enjoy the real play in all its rationalist
rigor. The theory was then reapplied to the plays with almost
pathological ingenuity, and with atrocious results. Thus Alkestis
never really died (for Euripides was too sensible to believe in
the nonsense of regeneration), while the great labors of Herakles and his harrowing of Hades were all fictive disguises for
the real tragedy of a great man who struggled, not under the
lash of a god-driven necessity, but merely with his own megalo-
mania. And so on, with hideous rigor of application, throughout
most of the Euripidean corpus.

Yet for all the visible absurdity of Verrall's conclusions, his
theory should command more respect than it does. At least
it seems to me both more perceptive and more courageous than
most Euripidean criticism with its outraged Aristotelian literal-
ness and its perpetual cry of formal botching and inconsistency.
Verrall's own mistake came, I think, not in his double-reality
pattern, but in the hypothesis which was meant to mirror what
he saw, that division of the play into two continuous levels of
action, real and apparent, each autonomous and complete. The
worst that can be said of Verrall's theory is that its elaboration

was first unnecessary and then untruthful; and in this it appears to me to resemble most critical theories which operate everywhere on the assumption of parallel levels of reality, or of real and apparent meanings. We need, I think, a greater sense of the variety of ways in which reality gets into literature, and I personally wish it were more often possible in contemporary criticism to preserve, for appropriate writers, the notion of reality as apparently fortuitous, and even casual, to keep respect for the simple, formal rightness of luck in things that happen. Verrall certainly had no such respect, and his criticism must pay the cost of a reality so terribly schematized as to be that much less a reality.

It should be obvious by now in what sense Verrall's theory of Euripidean structure is cautionary for Eliot. And perhaps it is too obvious, but in almost all the criticism of Eliot's two comedies with which I am familiar, the crucial difficulty has come in stating precisely just what relationship obtains between the secular framework of the plot and the constant hints of another, and Christian, reality. Are we meant to take the physical cocktail party as the empty vehicle of Christian communion? Do we have two continuous Verrallian "levels," one secular and one Christian? Or is the connection between the doublet reality of the play merely adventitious and momentary, a sudden irruption of the Christian real into the secular terms of the play, illuminating and transfiguring them?

Both Euripides and Eliot present in their plays a double reality, and a Euripidean play no more consists of an "ostensible" action superimposed on a "real" one than an Eliot play consists of one Christian and one secular action. The relation between the two realities is variously systematic and adventitious, and the term I suggest for their connection is that of "conversion"—if, for a moment, I can use the word without its religious connotations. By "conversion" I mean simply the transfiguration of one action or its terms, a conversion or transformation of one reality to another—but not an "epiphany" and not a conversion of "levels."

The commonest form of such conversion in Euripides is that in which a story (i. e., a *logos*) derived from received beliefs—the world of myth and the corpus of "things as they are said to be"—is suddenly, in all of its parts—its terms, its characters, and the values it invokes—"converted," under dramatic pressure, to another phase of reality. What we get is something like a dramatic mutation of conventional or traditional reality, and the leap the play makes between the phases or plateaus of its two realities is meant to correspond, in force and vividness and apparent unpredictability, to mutations in the physical world. It is this violence in the conversion of reality that explains the wrenching dislocation of Euripidean drama from an Aristotelian point of view, and the apparent lack of necessary connection between the parts of the play. The play pivots on two seemingly incompatible realities, and if it insists on the greater reality of what has been dramatically created over what has been traditionally received, it does not do so by denying validity to received reality, but subtly displaces it in the transfiguration of its terms. Euripidean structure mirrors in this way both the artist's intent and his possibilities. Because Euripides is dramatizing the incongruities of a culture—its received values against its actual or ideal values—he must at least allow dignity of reality to the values which the play supersedes. And at least one consequence of such a method is clearly psychological strain for his characters, who have to bear the intolerable burden of the cultural disparity which the play dramatizes. Thus in the *Orestes,* for instance, the matricide is presented in a world in which the institution of civil justice already exists, and, in consequence, Orestes' action exposes his own criminal nature, rather than being, as in the *Oresteia,* a god-driven deed which leads to the creation of civil justice.

In no play is this conversion of reality more sharp than in the *Herakles.* Here two savagely different actions, one conventional and the other set in a world where tradition is dumb and conduct uncharted, are jammed harshly against each other, and the collision of their values is stressed by the most violent peripety of Greek tragedy. The first action is static and conventional melodrama, wholly informed by "things as they are said to be," and rounded off with a cozy and traditionalized theodicy in which hybris is punished and virtue rewarded by the benevolent and vindicated gods. Herakles himself is presented essentially as Pindar had left him: the great culture-hero of enormous physical strength, self-sufficient and bearing on his back all the values of aristocratic *aretē.* His civilizing labors and his harrowing of Hades are accepted as literal truths, and the ambiguity in tradition which made Herakles the son of two fathers, Zeus and Amphitryon, is sustained.

Against such a background, the second action breaks with tragic force and striking transformations, showing first the conquering hero, the *kallinikos,* reduced to tears, helpless, dependent, and in love, stripped of that outward strength which until now had exempted him from normal human necessity, and discovering both his common ground with men and the internalized courage of the human hero confronting his condition. And point for point, each of the terms that was appropriate to the Herakles of tradition is transformed and displaced. Thus Amphitryon becomes Herakles' "real" father, not by the fact of conception, but by the fact of love, *philia,* while the literal descent to Hades is transformed in the refusal to die and the courage which, under an intolerable necessity, perseveres. The old Hades of the poets, with its Sisyphos, Cerberos, and torments, is transformed into the Hades within, here and now, as Herakles himself declares: "And I am like Ixion, chained forever to a flying wheel." So too the old labors are replaced by the metaphorical sense of the labors of human life and the cost of civilization, while the goddess Hera, who in myth made Herakles mad and the destroyer of his sons, demonstrates her own incredibility as a goddess and passes almost insensibly into a hovering symbol of all those irrational and random necessities which the Greeks and the play call *Tukhe,* and which we limply translate as "Fortune."

All these conversions replace and dislodge, but do not disown, the first action by transfiguring it at every point. The first action is neither false nor even unreal, but it is inadequate. Through the force of contrast with its own transfiguration it comes to seem obsolete, naive, or even humdrum, much as fresh conviction, formed under *peine forte et dure,* insensibly makes the conviction it replaces naive or jejune in comparison. Under the changed light of experience and the pattern it imposes, what was once taken for reality comes to seem illusion at best:

true while held as true, but with widened experience discovered inadequate. And what we see is less the contradiction between the two opposed realities than the counterpointed relation of their development, the way in which, under the blow of experience and insight, one reality is made to yield a further one, each geared to its appropriate experience. We begin with a familiar and conventional world, operating from familiar motives in a field of accepted, though outmoded, values; by the time the play closes, character, motives, and values have all been transfigured and pushed to the very frontiers of reality.

What Verrall saw with great clarity was the defeat of one reality by another in Euripides, and he correctly observed that the victorious reality was essentially a rationalized one. But because he assumed the connection between them was precisely that between false illusion and natural reality, rather than a series of discrete conversions, he stultified the plays and distorted their direction. He observed, that is, the rationalization of the fabulous and the outmoded or barbarous supernatural in Euripides; but he failed to notice that this rationalization was not final, that Euripides more often than not discredits the fabulous only in order to make it good, to re-earn it, on a symbolic or a metaphorical level. Illusion is not merely exposed, but it is first exposed and then transfigured or "converted." Thus Verrall rightly assumed that Euripides believed neither in Hades nor in the physical regeneration of Alkestis, but ignored the moral and metaphorical equivalent of her "death." For the point of the *Alkestis* is surely not, as Verrall thought, that Alkestis neither really died nor went to Hades, but that she had to "die" if Admetos, and hence herself, were ever to be "reborn." But as Eliot saw and put it in *The Cocktail Party,* the crux of the *Alkestis* is, after all, that moral death is the condition of moral rebirth; that Admetos (like Edward) must, even at the risk of apparent weakness, take back his wife from Herakles' hands as a new woman or not at all. But, obsessed by his own rationalist convictions and encouraged by Euripides' clear commitment to *this* world, Verrall imposed upon the plays a crude rationalism foreign to them, and he distorted their structure accordingly.

Between Euripides and Verrall, then, there is some small common ground in an initial rationalism; and while structurally Euripides does possess a doublet-reality, his plays are actually not doublet on two levels but complex conversions. Between Euripides and Eliot, there is, I hope to show, a common technique of transfiguration, though in Eliot the conversion is differently directed. But I should like now to raise the question as to whether Eliot, intending a Christian play along the structural lines of a Euripidean conversion, has not in fact written a Verrallian two-level comedy, and done so under the duress of religious doctrine and poetic theory.

It is essentially a conversion like that of the *Herakles,* though differently oriented and more fortuitous, which I think Eliot's two comedies are intended to exhibit. Both Eliot and Euripides are in some sense dramatizing incongruities, either in a given culture or in their own souls, and both thereby place upon their characters an unnatural strain, a strain which makes Euripides' characters pathological and Eliot's either priggish or negative. And just as in Euripides the unity of the plays depends upon the perception of the conversion, so in Eliot, I think, the perceived

convergence of two worlds, the momentary poetic incarnation
of Christian reality, is meant to earn that stillness and serene
reconciliation which is the mark of Christian "comedy" from
Dante on. For to reconcile appearance and reality, the world of
men and the world of God, is to make a Christian peace between two intersecting orders at the moment of their intersec-
tion.

Thus the Christian component in Eliot's plays is not a profounder "level" but a world of greater reality intended, under the
pressure of poetry, to become incarnate in the secular terms of
the play. We should be just enough aware of it on the fringes
of our emotional field that we may sense or glimpse the transfiguration of the world of the play. Eliot has recently remarked
that poetry in the theater should be "a kind of humble shadow
or analogy of the Incarnation," and, in saying this, he merely
expresses his determination to adapt his technical means to
his subject. The more intense moments of the play, the moments
when reality breaks upon us, are precisely the moments of poetry:
only poetry could bear the intolerable weight of such a reality.
Thus the Christian real supervenes in poetry and transforms the
play and its persons, who are thereby "renewed, transfigured in
another pattern"—to borrow, for a moment, the language of
the *Quartets*.

This simple strategy of transfiguration is not, of course, new
to Eliot; it runs throughout both his criticism and the late poetry.
But it has nonetheless visibly put off critics accustomed to
Eliot's tight metaphorical and symbolic allusiveness and his old
complexity of reference. For this technique does not "refer"
nor is it properly symbolic at all, but opencast, receptive rather

than referring, and more like revelation in action than a symbolic *déjà-vue*. Eliot's clearest statement of his intentions is to be found in an old (1934) essay on John Marston, which deserves, I think, being savored:

> It is possible that what distinguishes poetic drama from prosaic drama is a kind of doubleness of action, as if it took place on two planes at once. In this it is different from allegory, in which abstraction is something conceived, not something differently felt, and from symbolism, in which the tangible world is visibly diminished. . . . both symbolism and allegory being operations of the conscious planning mind. In poetic drama, a certain apparent irrelevance may be the symptom of this doubleness; or the drama has an underpattern, less manifest than the theatrical one. We sometimes feel, in following the words and behaviour of some of the characters of Dostoevsky, that they are living at once on the plane that we know and on some other plane of reality from which we are shut out: their behaviour does not seem crazy, but rather in conformity with the laws of some other world that we cannot perceive.

How closely that comment on Dostoyevsky parallels the experience of audiences and critics alike with both of Eliot's comedies hardly needs comment, though whether the effect is the same, or the primary realities equal, is a more serious question. More important to observe, I think, is the fact that, besides intending transfiguration, Eliot also intended that transfiguration to be precisely teasing, unanchored, and directly suggestive of the mystery it was meant to record. And for this reason, any attempt to state, rather than to suggest, the quality of conversion and to isolate a particular reference from among the body of invoked possibilities risks the pedantry of naming the unnamable.

Let me therefore risk it. For it seems to me that one of the most damning things about Eliot's comedies is the degree to which these mysteries are structured and the plays sacrificed to them, artificialized in order to make the advent of reality appear fortuitous. We have, that is, the spectacle of verse drama in which cool strategy and an old poetic ontology dictate that the only use of heightened language shall be to trap the Christian reality in the humdrum secular and quasi-prosaic world. Consider Eliot's own words in his essay, *Poetry and Drama:*

> It seems to me that beyond the namable, classifiable emotions and motives of our conscious life when directed towards action—the part of life which prose drama is wholly adequate to express—there is a fringe of indefinite extent, of feeling which we can only detect, so to speak, out of the corner of the eye and can never completely focus; of feeling of which we are only aware in a kind of temporary detachment from action . . . This peculiar range of sensibility can be expressed by dramatic poetry, at its moments of greatest intensity.

This fringe on which we can never wholly focus is, in Eliot's practice, almost entirely Christian; and I suppose no focus is possible precisely because it is Christian, a reality beyond the focusing, naming, and referring power of language geared to the lower reality of the world. And if the province of poetry in

Eliot's comedies is thus explicitly Christian, the ordinary world and its illusions receive the doubtful benefits of Eliot's humdrum business-verse. Sir Claude Mulhammer says it all apropos of his pots:

> To be among such things,
> If it is an escape, is escape into living,
> Escape from a sordid world into a pure one.
> Sculpture and painting—I have some good things—
> But they haven't this . . . remoteness I have always
>   longed for.
> I want a world where the form is the reality,   .
> Of which the substantial is only a shadow.

Where ceramics are in question, Sir Claude is almost a pure Platonist, and what he says of his pots is almost identical with what Eliot says elsewhere (*The Aims of Poetic Drama*) of his use of poetry and prose in the theater:

> What I should like to do is this: that the people on the stage should seem to the audience so like themselves that they would find themselves thinking: "I could talk in poetry too!" Then they are not transported into an unaccustomed, artificial world; but their ordinary, sordid world is suddenly illuminated and transfigured. And if poetry cannot do that for people, it is merely a superfluous decoration.

Poetry in Eliot's two comedies is thus reserved for the contemplation of the Christian idea, as it transfigures the sordid phenomenal reality of the lower half of the Platonic Line, the region of prosaic drama, or prosaic verse.

For Plato, the crucial difficulty with the Theory of Ideas was the difficulty of stating, other than metaphorically, just how the Ideas participated in the particulars they subsumed. And the classic objection against the Theory of Ideas is that, although it began as an attempt to explain the phenomenal world, it ended not in explaining it but simply in duplicating it. For Eliot the problem is altered, not merely because Eliot is a Christian and Christians solved Plato's difficulty by declaring the Incarnation a mystery and so putting it philosophically out of bounds, but because, in dramatic poetry, the only test is really a pragmatic one: is "our ordinary, sordid world" transfigured, or is it not? In asking this question, I do not think we are entitled to object that we are quite content with ordinary reality, or that it is not as sordid as Eliot appears to think. Certainly I have no wish that my own sordid reality should be transfigured as that of the Mulhammers was, but I am anxious that the question of belief in poetry should not be raised here. The questions which I should like to raise are these: First, is it really true that, if poetry does not transfigure ordinary reality, it must be merely "superfluous decoration"? Second, is it possible to transfigure something which, properly speaking, has no figuration in dramatic reality at all? And finally, to what extent is Eliot's all-important assumption, that Christianity is, on the level of dramatic popularity, operative enough to bear this opencast transfiguration and still remain recognizably Christian, a delusion?

Before attempting to answer these questions, let me first try to give particularity to the separate transfigurations as they occur in the plays. Many of them are extremely obvious, perhaps most of them; but, since the play is constructed for them, and is hopelessly diminished if they go unperceived, it is best that they submit to temporary prose impoverishment. As plots, both plays essentially contain a full conversion—and I mean here literal Christian conversion—from the secular to the Christian life. The Christianity of the characters may be fully conscious, as in Eggerson, or conscious but disguised for evangelical purposes as in the Guardians, or effective but inarticulate, as in the Chamberlaynes and Lucasta and Barnabas Kaghan (if I may give him his Christian name), or incipient and transcendent, a gift of the Spirit, as in Celia and Colby. All of the characters suffer their conversion into Christian life as their abilities and their spiritual gifts allow. Further, since each convert dies to be reborn, the coda of each play contains the familiar shadow analogy of the rite of rebirth, the death of the secular self and the putting on of the new Adam in the adoption of God. This conversion, so far as the double reality of the play is concerned, means also reconciliation and convergence: the awful gap between two apparently disparate orders, happily and comically intersecting, closes in the dedication to others which signifies the death of the desiring and worldly self. In the language of the *Quartets* again:

> See, now they vanish,
> The faces and places, with the self which, as it could,
>   loved them,
> To become renewed, transfigured, in another pattern.

In this final reconciliation, there is meant to emerge into familiar outline the whole foreshadowed, hinted pattern of the Christian life: church, martyrdom, Easter, *caritas,* the perpetual conspiracy, and the life of Christ informing the lives of men. Thus the Guardians leave Edward and Lavinia as Guardians of Peter, leave for a new "cocktail party" at the Gunnings, and a new communion after a fresh conversion. In *The Confidential Clerk* the conversion is less overt, though more explosive. Eggerson mentions, *en passant,* that his wife gets low-spirited "around this season When we're getting near the anniversary." "The anniversary?" asks Sir Claude, "Of your son's death?" and Eggerson replies, dodging the death of *his* son in order to suggest the Good Friday death of The Son, "Of the day we got the news." And hard on the heels of that death comes of course the Easter of conversion, the birth of Christ in the lives of the *dramatis personae:* enter Athene Guzzard, *dea ex machina,* like a grizzled Easter rabbit, to hand out new lives all around. Down in Joshua Park, the lilies should be in bloom.

This final convergence of the play's double reality is foreshadowed in detail in the isolated transfigurations of the plays. Thus the cocktail party is transformed into the Eucharist, and the conversion is given point in the pure Pentecostal water which the subapostolic Sir Henry drinks—unadulterated with gin—when he is not in his secular disguise. The indefinable aura of divinity and power which attaches to the Guardians finds its source in the divinity of the Christian life itself, which informs their undisclosed conspiracy of conversion. So too, when Colby rejects Sir Claude and Lady Elizabeth he insensibly, and yet, I think, clearly, paraphrases Scripture: we know he is about his "father's business." The play's worldly quest of fathers seeking sons and sons seeking fathers is perfected and transfigured in the adoption of God ("ye have received the spirit of adoption

whereby we cry, Abba, Father!"); and the doctrine of Original
Sin transfigures Sir Claude's lifelong atonement to a father. Behind the concern with the professions and the vocations lie the
greatest Vocation and the gifts of the Spirit, and with the loss
of worldly love and ambitions, comes *caritas,* the greatest of the
Gifts and the enabling condition of the others. "All that's left
is love," says Colby, echoing Paul. He means, of course, worldly
love transfigured, "expansion of love beyond desire," the same
love that marks the putting on of the new man and the release of the individual and his lesser gifts from the private
garden of the self into the service of others and of God. It is
with "the drawing of the Love and the voice of this Calling,"
that conversion can come and Christian reality supervene. Thus
the problem of the individual is also the problem of the play:
to effect a reconciliation between appearance and reality, to find
unity by discovering God and others walking in one's private
garden.

"What is the reality of experience between two unreal people?"
asks Peter in *The Cocktail Party,* and the answer of both plays
is that unreality is at least partly redeemed by the release of the
individual into the shared reality of "the body of Christ." "It
may be," says Lucasta to Colby, "there's no one so hard to understand As one's brother . . ." and she speaks, of course, of her
brother by Adoption: "whosoever shall do the will of God, the
same is my brother, and my sister, and mother." Both plays
again, without overt consciousness of doctrine, dramatize the
famous dualism of the orthodox confession, the life lived according to the Counsels and that according to the Precepts. The
Counsels of Perfection are represented in the celibate choices

of Celia and Colby, while the Precepts inform the lives of all others, even Eggerson and the Guardians. So Eggerson, and latterly Colby, carry with them, as confidential clerks, Christian *fides,* the substance of things hoped for, the evidence of things unseen. And so on, term for term, throughout both comedies, a series of discrete conversions whose cumulative effect is to bring closer and closer together, in preparation for the final convergence of conversion, the two realities of the plays.

Something like this, with the Christian reality enhanced by being made less explicit and evoked vividly in poetic incarnation, is, I submit, the intent of both comedies. If there is an intent beyond this, it can only be, I think, the conversion (or reconversion) of an audience at least unconsciously Christian—an audience sufficiently at home in the reach-me-down world of Christian habits and terms that the reality of Christian experience can be at least partially restored to them by playing over the fringes of the emotional field, hinting and suggesting, but not evangelizing. Such audience conversion is also the aim of Euripidean drama, but in Euripides, so far as I can judge, the premises on which the conversion rests are better founded on fact and better supported by dramatic genius. That is, the values which Euripides assumes and invokes against received values are clearly operative, even on the popular level of the theater; and further, their effective operation on received material is earned through absolute control of the techniques of persuasion and extraordinary ingenuity in the enlisting and alienation of sympathies.

But with Eliot I am skeptical of the validity of the premises and puzzled in general to know just how he expects any conceivable *popular* modern audience to respond to these transfigurations. For Christian reality looks to me (from the outside) like an extraordinarily complex one, in which understanding of the part is inevitably dependent upon understanding of the whole, or the parts at least mutually illuminate one another. What puzzles me then is to know just how a mystery can be invoked or transfigured, with the richness of its own reality, unless it has the precision of a mystery. There are, after all, mysteries and mysteries: Greek is regrettably a mystery for those who do not know it, but the Incarnation is a mystery even to those who know all there is to know about it. And if my own estimate of the experience of those conventional, unconscious, or merely habitual Christians who saw either of Eliot's comedies is correct, then what they saw was a mystery analogous to the mystery of Greek for the Greekless. They came away in impure puzzlement, aware that something profound, even something Christian, was taking place in the plays, something just outside their ken, teasing and indefinable; but finally, no more interesting than the mysteries of Greek for a practical man. Reality was observed, even felt, and felt, as Eliot wanted, hovering on the fringes of the mind's eye, but for all that utterly unrealized; and so too transfiguration was observed dimly as it broke, but yet there was no transfiguration.

Now, in part, this reaction was what Eliot intended, that the plays should be both teasing and unsettling; but he also intended that they should be evocative and finally satisfying, and in this last he seems to me to have badly miscarried. For what, after all, are the perceptions of the adoption of God or the Incarnation worth unless they are perceived, as mysteries, in the richness of their Christian reality? What can you do with the adoption of

God unless you have a belief which illuminates it and a context which can place it? What do the "counsels of perfection" mean to those sub-Christians who live the precepts by force of habit or discipline and have neither knowledge nor tolerance of any other way? What can Colby possibly be, except a prig or a musical eunuch, unless you have the *Ion* to tell you of his musical father, Apollo, and a Christian education to tell you what his Vocation is?

Eliot, that is, appears to me to want it both ways: he wants the precision and richness and reality of Christian doctrine and mystery in order to make his play finally a true comedy of reconciliation, to elicit a genuine order, complete at every point, from the secular disorder with which he begins. But he also wants that evocative power that comes from a mystery comprehended vaguely or not at all, the teasing power of a "plane of reality from which we are shut out." He is, of course, welcome to both, but at least one of the consequences of having them both is that of writing Verrallian double-level comedy: one play, a well-made farce with Christian overtones, and another play, a complete Christian comedy, superimposed, like the *Clementine Homilies,* on a Greek romance and available only to educated Christians or to meddlers like myself. All probability, I think, so far as intent is concerned, opposes the Verrallian interpretation, as do Eliot's own words; and I can only suppose that Eliot has, with good Christian confidence, misjudged the potential Christianity of his popular audience. If he has not misjudged his audience, he has, in good faith, overestimated the power of Christian mysteries to reveal themselves to those who have lost the secrets of their own initiation. For unless the audience feels

that the world of the play, and itself with it, has been even mo-
mentarily transfigured, and feels it at a profounder depth than
that of a mild secular puzzlement, it is hard to see that any
transfiguration at all has taken place. Rather, the play will have
transfigured "ordinary, sordid" reality only by artificializing it
into a rather puzzling, though well-made, wish-fulfillment.

Alternatively, the failure may lie less in doctrine and the
strategies of an audience than in the technique of transfiguration itself. Is it, after all, possible to transfigure what has, dramatically, no real figuration of its own? If the relation between
father and son, or between lovers, is not, as the world goes and
as poetry goes, made real, what happens to the Christian love
that is meant to transfigure it? In asking this question, I am
trying to suggest that the ontology of Eliot's poetry and his own
special version of Christianity is dramatically doomed from the
start: the stage, as Plato himself suggested when he destroyed
his own tragedies, is no place for Platonists, or for gnostics, or
for the theologian of the *Four Quartets*.

For two reasons—his own doctrine of negative transcendence
and his gnostic distinction between prose and poetry—Eliot has
made a desolation and called it the world. In both of these plays,
and even more acutely in *The Confidential Clerk* than in *The
Cocktail Party,* the world has been stultified to such a degree
that the intended transfiguration is belittled even before it is
begun. There is so little here to be transfigured. And just as it
is the greatest sinners who make, at least in drama, the most
interesting saints, so I should have supposed it was the liveliest
illusions that got themselves most firmly transfigured. What we
have instead is the spectacle of religious, without dramatic,

redemption; of the new man without the old Adam; of transfigured love without the love it was transfigured from. Yet it stands to reason that illumination requires a darkness to dispel, just as Incarnation needs a world of flesh. Here the illusions of the world are allowed almost no dignity whatsoever. How easily, in *The Cocktail Party,* people surrender their selves, their passions, and their identities. How little is required in *The Confidential Clerk* to make a man surrender his illusion of parental love. How little dignity of language these people have in which to report the love and grief we are meant to credit them with. It is exactly because the illusions of this world are left without real dignity that the loss of illusions fails to matter. And yet it is through the loss of their worldly illusions and ambitions that these characters are meant to come upon their Christian reality.

Given Eliot's rather special version of Christianity, this impoverishment of the world was either necessary or natural. You cannot quarrel with a man who makes a desolation of the world as a matter of principle. Yet one reason, I think, why Eliot's two comedies fail where his poetry succeeds is that he has been unable to find the dramatic equivalent of that terrible poetic reality of unreality which is so vivid in the *Quartets:* "Not here, not here, the darkness, in this twittering world." You can't beat a twitter like that for realizing the unreal, but if its dramatic equivalent is Lady Elizabeth's

> Why, I'd no sooner got to Lausanne
> Than whom should I meet but Mildred Deverell.
> She was going to Zurich. So she said "Come to Zurich!

There's a wonderful doctor who teaches mind control."
So on I went to Zurich,

or even the fine chatter from the first scene of *The Cocktail
Party*, or the pallid suffering of Edward and Lavinia or the
incipient passion of Colby and Lucasta, then Eliot is merely
mocking, not creating, the terms he intends to transfigure,
stripping them of the dignity they need in order to carry their
conversion.

A few lines back, I deliberately introduced the phrase "the
poetic reality of unreality" to indicate the point at which Plato-
nism in poetry declares itself bankrupt. Ordinarily I dislike such
phrases, but I want, even by paradox, to expose what I take to
be the misplaced ontology of Eliot's poetic and dramatic practice. As a Christian, Eliot perhaps distinguishes between two
worlds in terms of a greater and a lesser reality. But as a poet he
makes such a distinction at his peril and also at the peril of his
Christian reality. Poetry may, with perfect propriety, be made
the servant of Christianity, but to suppose that this privileged
service is therefore exclusive of any other seems to me dramatic
and poetic suicide. From the fact that Eliot dooms this world
to a diminished reality, it hardly follows that the world must
also be doomed to diminished poetry. To suppose that it does
follow, deprives poetry of all its multifariousness, its disguises,
and its very ability to transfigure. For you cannot transform a
vacuum except into a purer one; you cannot worthily redeem
what is not worth redemption, and so too you cannot make the
world declare the glory, or even the greater glory, of God unless
you give it some glory to begin with. And what is true of language is true also of men and their illusions of reality in this

world. Christianity may, though it need not, suggest that the passage from the world to the spirit is via the way of deprivation, and poetry will guarantee the dignity of that passage by making the experience of deprivation a real one. But to suppose that you get to *caritas* by being only a limp poet in love and thus easily deprived of your small purchase on the world is a strategy whose folly is equaled only by supposing that Christian poetry exhibits its reality best when transfiguring secular prose. The victory is too easy. For a playwright who happens to be both a poet and a Christian, the true test in drama of both faith and poetry would have been, I think, to realize his reality wherever he could, and to have trusted in the greater richness of his Christianity to earn its triumph over the best the world might offer.

In closing, let me briefly set against Eliot's relative failure the example of Euripides, a dramatist who everywhere took the full risks of his convictions and his verse. In play after play occur systematic transfigurations analogous to those intended by Eliot: from a lesser to a greater reality, from a familiar world to an unfamiliar one. But, unlike Eliot, Euripides consistently gives the fullest play of his poetic powers, not to his final transfiguring reality, but to the reality that gets transfigured. Thus in the *Elektra,* a conversion play designed to make the monstrous acquire mercy, everything has been given to the deed—the matricide—which the play is written to execrate, as the new Euripidean imperative of pity dislodges, or perfects, the old Aeschylean ordinance of civil justice. Orestes and Elektra, old heroes become new criminals, are invested with poetry in the full flush of power, with the whole catalogue of heroic myth and the panoply of tradition, with all metaphor and all sympathy. Far from diluting their reality, Euripides intensifies it, and then, set-ting action against words, he terribly exploits and undoes all the reality he has created. The undoing is, of course, not gratuitous; it is the condition of the conversion and the emergence of pity as the informing law which the play tragically creates. So too in the *Herakles,* the traditional figuration of the hero's greatness is given resonance in a massively powerful dirge which wheels for a hundred lines through the canonical Twelve Labors, earn-ing reality for an image of the hero which the play's second action annuls. For the close of the play is a conversion in which Herakles is reduced, but also raised, to the human condition, and his old heroism transfigured in the perfected humanity of the hero. Or think again of the overwhelming loveliness of lan-guage and ecstasy which the *Bakkhai* gives to the chorus, before revealing its hideous depravity; or of the precariously tender sleep scene of the *Orestes,* which enhances the hero admired of tradi-tion before the sudden revelation of his terrible brutality.

In all of these plays, reality of poetry or of passion or of situa-tion is the indispensable condition of conversion. What the play will finally disclose as illusion is treated as fully real until the very moment of disclosure. In this way, Euripides, as against Eliot, earns his transfiguration by making his poetry the test of its own truth and the stumbling-block that it imposes on itself; he allows illusion to claim the status and dignity of reality until transfigured and exposed for what it is. Until Mr. Eliot, I think, is willing once more to take the risk of his own gift of tongues and to accept, at least dramatically, the reality of illusion in this world, his own calling cannot be higher than that of a dramatist without compelling Vocation.

ᵛᵍ THE ENGLISH INSTITUTE PROGRAM

September 13 through September 17, 1954

Conferences

I. EDITORIAL PROBLEMS IN SHAKESPEARE
   Directed by CHARLTON HINMAN, *Folger Shakespeare Library*

   1. Semi-Popular Editions of Shakespeare
      ARTHUR BROWN, *University College, London*

   2. Compositor Determination and Related Problems
      ALICE WALKER, *Welcombe, Devonshire*

   3. New Approaches to Textual Problems in Shakespeare
      PHILIP WILLIAMS, *University of Virginia*

   4. McKerrow's Editorial Principles Reconsidered
      FREDSON BOWERS, *University of Virginia*

II. TRANSLATORS ON TRANSLATING
    Directed by REUBEN A. BROWER, *Harvard University*

    1. On Translating Greek Poetry
       RICHMOND LATTIMORE, *Bryn Mawr College*

2. The Art of Translation (with Examples from Russian)
   VLADIMIR NABOKOV, *Cornell University*

3. From French to English
   JUSTIN O'BRIEN, *Columbia University*

4. Rhyming Dante in English
   JOHN CIARDI, *Rutgers University*

III. THE POETICS OF FRENCH SYMBOLISM
   Directed by HARRY LEVIN, *Harvard University*

   1. Baudelaire
      JUDD D. HUBERT, *Harvard University*

   2. Mallarmé
      WARREN RAMSEY, *University of California*

   3. Rimbaud
      WILBUR M. FROHOCK, *Wesleyan University*

   4. Valéry
      JACKSON MATHEWS, *University of Washington*

IV. ENGLISH STAGE COMEDY
   Directed by W. K. WIMSATT, JR., *Yale University*

   1. Shakespeare's *Tempest* and the Ancient Comic Tradition
      BERNARD KNOX, *Yale University*

   2. Unifying Symbols in the Comedy of Ben Jonson
      RAY L. HEFFNER, JR., *Indiana University*

3. Restoration Comedy and Later
   MARVIN MUDRICK, *Santa Barbara College*

4. The Comedy of T. S. Eliot
   WILLIAM ARROWSMITH, *Wesleyan University*

Evening Meetings

SEPTEMBER 14

The Nature and Limits of Aesthetic Autonomy
JOHN E. SMITH, *Yale University*

SEPTEMBER 16

The Formation of the Modern Literary Public in Europe
ERICH AUERBACH, *Yale University*

Reverend Edward E. Aksomaitis, Marianapolis Preparatory School; Gellert S. Alleman, Rutgers University at Newark; H. P. Allen; Judith Hill Allgood, New York University; Catherine L. Almirall, Columbia University; Russell K. Alspach, United States Military Academy; G. L. Anderson, University of Maryland; Marcia Lee Anderson, Asheville-Biltmore College; Constance Veysey Apperman, Hunter College; Mother Thomas Aquinas, College of New Rochelle; George Arms, University of New Mexico; Erich Auerbach, Yale University; William Arrowsmith, Wesleyan University; James Baird, Connecticut College; C. L. Barber, Amherst College; Richard K. Barksdale, North Carolina College at Durham; Josephine Waters Bennett, Hunter College; Alice R. Bensen, Michigan State Normal College; Raymond A. Biswanger, Jr., University of Georgia; Maria P. Bizzoni, Morehead State College; Matthew W. Black, University of Pennsylvania; Thomas A. Bledsoe, Alfred A. Knopf; Andrew Bongiorno, Oberlin College; Edward E. Bostetter, University of Washington; Brother C. Francis Bowers, Catholic University; Fredson Bowers, University of Virginia; Evelyn Mae Boyd, Grinnell College; Cleanth Brooks, Yale University; Reuben A. Brower, Harvard University; Arthur

Brown, University College, London; Margaret M. Bryant, Brooklyn College; Albert H. Buford; Richard Burgi, Yale University; Brother Fidelian Burke, Catholic University; Arthur Burkhard; Glenn S. Burne, University of Washington; Sister M. Vincentia Burns, Albertus Magnus College.

Hugh C. G. Chase; John Ciardi, Rutgers University; James L. Clifford, Columbia University; William B. Coley, Wesleyan University; Francis X. Connolly, Fordham University; David K. Cornelius, Randolph-Macon Woman's College; Lucille Crighton, Gulf Park College; J. V. Cunningham, Brandeis University; Curtis Dahl, Wheaton College; Giles Dawson, Folger Shakespeare Library; Robert M. Dell, Pace College; Rutherford E. Delmage, St. Lawrence University; Sister Rose Bernard Donna, College of Saint Rose; Elizabeth Drew, Smith College; William Elton, Ohio State University; David V. Erdman, University of Minnesota; Charles Kenneth Eves, City College, New York; Joseph J. Firebaugh, Queens College; Ruth M. Fisher, Cornell University; Edward G. Fletcher, University of Texas; F. Cudworth Flint, Dartmouth College; Claude R. Flory, Florida State University; Frances A. Foster, Vassar College; Vincent Freimarck, Harpur College; Wilbur Frohock, Wesleyan University; Northrop Frye, Victoria College, University of Toronto; W. Todd Furniss, Ohio State University; Paul Fussell, Connecticut College; Katherine Haynes Gatch, Hunter College; Courtenay D. Gentry, Columbia University; Mary E. Giffin, Vassar College; Elaine Goldman Gill, Columbia University; Sister Mary Cyrille Gill, Rosary College; John W. Graham, University of Western Ontario.

V. B. Halpert, Polytechnic Institute of Brooklyn; Victor M.

Hamm, Marquette University; Thomas R. Hart, Jr., Harvard University; William Haskins, University of Chicago; Ihab H. Hassan, Wesleyan University; A. T. Hazen, Columbia University; Ray L. Heffner, Jr., Indiana University; Charles A. Herring, University of Virginia; Charlton Hinman, Folger Shakespeare Library; Daniel G. Hoffman, Columbia University; Joyce M. Horner, Mount Holyoke College; Richard Hosley, University of Virginia; Judd D. Hubert, Harvard University; Edward Hubler, Princeton University; Muriel J. Hughes, University of Vermont; Thomas C. Izard, Columbia University; Mackie L. Jarrell, Connecticut College; Lisle C. John, Hunter College; S. F. Johnson, Columbia University; Ralph James Kaufmann, Wesleyan University; Leo Kirschbaum, Wayne University; Mrs. Rudolf Kirk, Rutgers University; Slava Klima, Yale University; C. F. Klinck, University of Western Ontario; Bernard Knox, Yale University; Frank A. Krutzke, Colorado College; Reinhard C. Kuhn, Princeton University; George Kummer, Western Reserve University; James Craig La Drière, Catholic University; Seymour Lainoff, Yeshiva University; Lauriat Lane, Jr., Cornell University; Richmond Lattimore, Bryn Mawr; Natalie Grimes Lawrence, University of Miami; Lewis Leary, Columbia University; Carl Lefevre, Pace College; Leo Lemaire, Pace College; Harry Levin, Harvard University; Stanley Linder, Columbia University; Jean S. Lindsay, Hunter College; Julian Ira Lindsay, University of Vermont; Anne H. Littlefield, Russell Sage College; George deF. Lord, Yale University; Reverend William F. Lynch, Fordham University.

Marion K. Mabey, Fairleigh Dickinson College; George McFadden, Duquesne University; Kenneth MacLean, Victoria

College, University of Toronto; Helen N. McMaster, Sarah Lawrence College; E. Wallace McMullen, United States Department of Defense; Mother C. E. Maguire, Newton College of the Sacred Heart; Mother Mary Denis Mahoney, College of New Rochelle; Elizabeth L. Mann, Adelphi College; Emerson R. Marks, Rutgers University; Mary H. Marshall, Syracuse University; Thomas F. Marshall, Western Maryland College; Harold C. Martin, Harvard University; Aida Mastrangelo, Catholic University; Dorothy Mateer, College of Wooster; Jackson Mathews, University of Washington; Merrill M. May, Purdue University; Paul E. Memmo, Jr., Fordham University; Vivian H. S. Mercier, City College, New York; Milton Millhauser, University of Bridgeport; Louie M. Miner, Brooklyn College; Carlisle Moore, University of Oregon; Marvin Mudrick, Santa Barbara College; Vladimir Nabokov, Cornell University; Norman Nathan, Utica College of Syracuse University; Elizabeth Nitchie, Goucher College; Reverend William T. Noon, Canisius College; Martin K. Nurmi, University of North Dakota; Justin O'Brien, Columbia University; Pauline Wiggins O'Brien; James M. Osborn, Yale University; Louise B. Osborn, Central High School, Evansville, Ind.

Norman H. Pearson, Yale University; Harry William Pedicord, University of Pennsylvania; Allen W. Phillips, University of Michigan; Abbie F. Potts, Rockford College; Robert Preyer, Smith College; Strother B. Purdy, Columbia University; Reverend C. J. Quirk, Loyola University of the South; Warren Ramsey, University of California; Sister Mary Robert Reddy, College of Saint Rose; Mrs. Jonathan T. Rorer; H. Blair Rouse, Emory University; James U. Rundle, American Book Company; B. N. Schilling, University of Rochester; Helene B. M. Schnabel; Flora Rheta Schreiber, New School for Social Research; Helen M. Scurr, University of Bridgeport; Melvin Seiden, Carleton College; Robert G. Shedd, Ohio State University; Norman Silverstein, Queens College; John E. Smith, Yale University; Mother M. G. Smith, Newton College of the Sacred Heart; John Stafford, Brooklyn College; Nathan C. Starr, University of Florida; Jess Stein, Random House; Helen Larson Stevens, Illinois Institute of Technology; David L. Stevenson, Western Reserve University; Rosanne Stoesser, University of California; Samuel E. Stokes, Jr., Amherst College; Wylie Sypher, Simmons College.

Bryce Thomas, Pace College; Sidney Thomas, Queens College; Craig R. Thompson, Lawrence College; Doris Stevens Thompson, Russell Sage College; A. R. Towers, Jr., Princeton University; Alberta Turner, Oberlin College; W. Arthur Turner, Oberlin College; Rosemond Tuve, Connecticut College; Dale Underwood, Yale University; David M. Vieth, Yale University; Willis Wager, Boston University; Richard Waidelich, Goucher College; Eugene M. Waith, Yale University; John Waldron, Georgetown University; Alice Walker; Alba H. Warren, Jr.; René Wellek, Yale University; Reverend Norman Weyand, Loyola University; Charles B. Wheeler, Ohio State University; Philip Wheelwright, University of California, Riverside; Anne B. Whitmer, Ohio State University; Philip Williams, University of Virginia; Edwin E. Willoughby, Folger Shakespeare Library; W. K. Wimsatt, Jr., Yale University; Marion Witt, Hunter College.